# Adobe and Rammed Earth Buildings

A ten-story apartment house in South Yemen, built of earth. Extremely high compressive loads have caused crushing and sagging at the lower left in one building in the center. Note that windows are smaller and fewer at the lower part of the structure, in conformance with suggested engineering principles in Chapter 13. [Photo courtesy Centre de Documentation Photographiques sur l'Architecture. Photographies de Christin Bastin et Jacques Evrard, 127 rue de l'Arbre Benit, 1050 Brussels, Belgium.]

# Adobe and Rammed Earth Buildings

## design and construction

**Paul Graham McHenry, Jr. AIA**

ARCHITECT, ALBUQUERQUE, NEW MEXICO

*Chapter 13, Structural Engineering for Earth Buildings by*

**Gerald W. May, Ph.D.**

DEAN, COLLEGE OF ENGINEERING
UNIVERSITY OF NEW MEXICO

**A Wiley-Interscience Publication**
**JOHN WILEY & SONS**
New York    Chichester    Brisbane    Toronto    Singapore

*Library of Congress Cataloging in Publication Data*

McHenry, Paul Graham.
  Adobe and rammed earth buildings.

  "A Wiley-Interscience publication."
  Includes index.
  1. Building, Adobe.  2. Earth houses.  I. Title.

TH4818.A3M3  1983        693′.22        83-10397
ISBN 0-471-87677-1

Printed in the United States of America

10 9 8 7 6 5 4 3 2 1

*This book is dedicated to all the architects, builders, and adoberos who unstintingly shared their many years of experience with me, and to my family, who encouraged me and gave up many weekends and holidays so it could be written. Special thanks must go to Thomas L. Lucero, architect, who prepared the excellent line drawings and illustrations. My sons, Bruce and Jamie, were also instrumental in its preparation—Bruce working many hours in the darkroom taking and processing photographs, and Jamie offering keen insight and suggestions. Last, but certainly not least, acknowledgment must go to my wife, Carol, who translated my terrible handwriting into typewritten manuscript.*

# Preface

Earth is the oldest building material used by humans and is the ultimate expression of appropriate technology. We are just now beginning to define the technology in scientific and engineering terms.

The purpose of this book is to establish the engineering logic for the various technologies that prevail and separate them from the folktales and traditional practices which may be valid only in certain circumstances. Hopefully, the information presented will allow the reader to draw logical conclusions, based on engineering principles and applied to the varying conditions of any particular location.

The technology of building with earth was developed by trial and error from the earliest beginnings of humankind. Necessity, time, and readily available materials were the principal ingredients in its development. Humans, with their native ingenuity, developed forms for its utilization that ranged from the very simple to the incredibly complex, and which were adapted to the particular environment in which they lived. All shelter was, and should be, a manifestation of appropriate technology, tempered by climatological conditions and ethnic background. Appropriate architecture should include the utilization of appropriate materials, and the form will be generated by the background of the builder.

Earth construction, in a wide variety of forms, is not only the oldest, but also the most widely used building material in the world today. More than 50% of the world's population today live in earthen houses. It was common in the United States 100 years ago, fairly widespread for rural schools and public buildings in the southwestern United States as little as 40 years ago, and is currently being ever more widely used for residential construction in nostalgic historical styles of the Southwest. Radical changes caused by the Industrial Revolution, cheap energy, and a rapid expansion of the transportation and distribution systems, in favor of more "modern" materials, had virtually eliminated the use of earth for building in the United States. In its forsaken state today, the earth construction skills that were common not too many years ago have been largely lost, or at least relegated to a small number of vernacular builders. These are mostly rural, often with little formal education, and a technology built on tradition rather than engineering. In most instances, the traditional technology has its roots in logical practices developed by trial and error. Cross-cultural influences and cultural migrations have resulted in vast confusion as to the valid engineering reasons for the details of the technology.

I designed and built my first adobe house more than 20 years ago, after a varied construction background of many years. Library research turned up little other than government pamphlets on farm buildings and an occasional owner builder record of the trials and tribulations of building one's own project. Building codes were limited or nonexistent on the subject, and lending institutions viewed any mud house with great suspicion. The big help came from the vernacular builders who built with their traditional practices, often differing greatly with those of other vernacular builders. The obvious conclusion from this investigation was that while each of the practitioners were sincere in his or her conclusions, the conclusions were based on experience in a limited geographical area. In one sense, each was right, at least to some degree, for the technology of a particular location. Each location had a different set of conditions.

The specifics and detailing of adobe and rammed earth wall construction are obviously different and will be dealt with separately. Other basic considerations such as foundations and roof structures have details that are common to both, so they will be dealt with as combination sections. Where differences occur, they are noted.

The word adobe is thought to be Arabic in origin, *atob*, meaning sticky paste or muck. Surprisingly, the word adobe is not used in the Middle East where the use of sun-dried mud brick seems to have started. In the southwestern United States, it has several meanings: A house of mud brick, a brick, or mud plaster. The word adobe must have come from North Africa through Spain to the New World. For our purposes here, the word adobe will refer to mud brick, rammed earth for itself, and earth wall for either.

Current energy costs and dwindling supplies of conventional materials make it logical to examine our basic energy costs. A substantial investment is made in creating the manufactured materials with which we may build. The most modern of these—aluminum, glass, concrete—represent enormous energy costs in the production of basic building materials, plus the cost of transportation to the building site from widely dispersed sources and central manufacturing locations. These considerations alone indicate that we should look backward in time to see how our predecessors dealt with the same problems we have today, but without the cheap energy supplies we have been squandering since their inception. It is my feeling that we have much to learn and gain from an examination of the past if we are able to put it into the proper perspective.

The preparation of this book represents the culmination of more than 20 years of research, field examination, trying ideas that worked, others that seemed logical but didn't work, and thoughtful reflection on the lessons learned from builders and craftsmen of several countries.

All photographs are by the author unless otherwise noted. Line drawings are by Thomas L. Lucero, Architect, and James G. McHenry.

**Paul Graham McHenry, Jr.**

*Albuquerque, New Mexico*
*June 1983*

# Contents

*chapter eight*
# Earth Wall Finishes    119

*chapter nine*
# Foundations    137

*chapter ten*
# Floor and Roof Structures    141

*chapter eleven*
# Insulation and Thermal Mass Values    153

*chapter twelve*

## Mechanical Considerations    165

*chapter thirteen*

## Structural Engineering for Earth Buildings    171

*chapter fourteen*

## Repair and Renovation of Earth Buildings    185

*chapter fifteen*

## Building Codes for Earth Construction    195

*appendix a*

## New Mexico Building Code for Adobe 1983    207

## chapter one

# History and Evolution of Earth Construction

The earliest beginnings of deliberately planned and built shelter were much the same in all parts of the world. Then, as now, there were many levels of development at any particular time, the level depending on the social evolution stage. These beginnings go back as far as the earliest archaeological investigations can take us, only the virtually indestructible stone tools remaining.

Humans, at the beginning stage of development, were constantly on the move, following hunting and gathering patterns dictated by the region in which they lived. The migratory nature of their subsistence made impossible the construction of a fixed dwelling place. As hunting and gathering patterns were refined, many of the more desirable locations (caves, cliff sites, with proximity to food and water) were revisited repeatedly. This was the beginning.

The earliest shelters using earth were outgrowths of temporary, seasonal shelters made of brush and small wood members, usually covered with mud for waterproofing. A common term for this type of construction is *jacal* (Fig. 1.1). Most activities took place out of doors, and shelter was for only the most inclement weather. Some physical details of the building design were for security from animals and hostile neighbors.

The possibility of obtaining and making use of larger structural members was dependent on the invention of tools with which to obtain them. Few tools other than sharp stones, a pointed stick, and the builder's hands were available. It was also necessary to have some method for carrying water to the construction site.

As human knowledge of agriculture increased to bring the level of culture from a hunter–gatherer phase to the more intensive cultivation of fixed locations, requirements for shelter increased as well. From a transient exis-

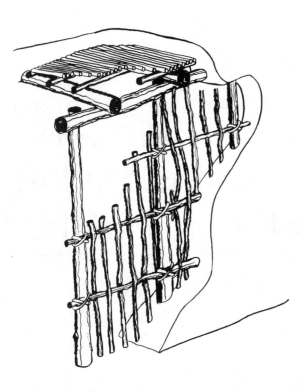

FIGURE 1.1. **Typical *jacal* construction. A wood framework is filled in and plastered with mud.**

tence which afforded little or no opportunity for a fixed dwelling place, humans learned to create surpluses of food and methods to store it. The surpluses created time and a desire for the development of more sophisticated forms of shelter. These first dwellings were partly underground, creating a sort of cave, a form which the builder was familiar with, and were called *pit houses.*

The pit house was, for the time, the ultimate in environmental design, appropriate technology, and labor economy. It made full use of materials close at hand, required little planning or preparation of the materials to be used. Various techniques of wall building were employed, including puddling of mud, lumps of mud, and a rudimentary type of brick formed in baskets, called *turtle* construction.

The pit house form used by the Hohokam irrigation farmers of the southwestern United States (100–900 A.D.) was so successful that it remained basically unchanged for more than 600 years (Fig. 1.2). Many of its features and principles are ones that we are rediscovering today, in the form of bermed and partially underground construction, taking refuge from the wind and collecting the sun warmth on protected south slopes.

While civilizations seem to have developed independently in many places on the globe, it progressed at different speeds, making it impossible to establish a firm chronologic period for specific stages of development on a global basis. Similar stages of construction technology often occurred centuries or even milleniums apart.

Variations in form and selection of materials was dependent on the local environment. Where stone was most readily available, it was used. Where wood and other organic materials were more abundant, they were used. In both cases, the use of earth was necessary to implement the other material. Where neither stone nor wood were abundant or viable, mud was used alone.

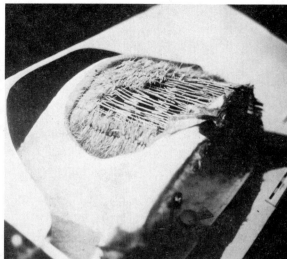

FIGURE 1.2. (*a*) **Typical pit house, cut-away section. This museum model is in the visitor center at Casa Grande National Monument, Casa Grande, Arizona.** (*b*) **Same, showing roof construction.**

FIGURE 1.3. **A farmhouse in England. This home is part adobe brick and part infill in a timber frame. Photo courtesy** *Adobe Today*, **Albuquerque, New Mexico.**

All three basic techniques are still being used in developing Third World countries.

Modern industrial countries today make some use of many of the basic techniques, more often in rural locations (Fig. 1.3).

The development of the (adobe) brick, a preformed modular masonry unit of sun-dried mud, occurred with higher civilization levels. Then, as now, the affluence of leisure time of the householder reflected itself in the material selection and architectural form, which in turn led to monumental forms for religious and public buildings (Fig. 1.4). Often crude forms and complex ones existed side by side, as they do today. The use of preformed bricks started

FIGURE 1.4. **A palace in Iran, 1972. This palace is being restored to its original splendor. Tall, slender wind towers are of adobe brick, a common feature in Iran for cooling and ventilation. Such heights for adobe masonry is prohibited by many U.S. building codes.**

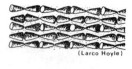

CONIQUE

PIRIFORME

HEMISPHERIQUE

DENTIFORME

FIGURE 1.5. **Shapes of mud bricks. Many sizes and shapes are found around the world, usually determined by local custom.** Courtesy *Construire en Terre*, Craterre, Grenoble, France.

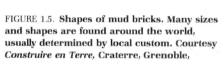

PLAN-CONVEXE

with a need for a more efficient, rapid construction technique, as the drying of puddled and shaped mud walls took a long time. Early forms of this are found in the southwestern United States where turtle wall construction occurred. In this form, mud was placed in a basket with a round bottom and either placed on the ground to dry, or laid directly up on the wall where it could dry in place. Other shapes are found worldwide (Fig. 1.5).

Another type of brick common in many areas is cut sod bricks. The Spanish name for this is *terrone*. These can be procured only in swampy, boggy river bottom lands. They are cut with a shovel from soil having a heavy grass root structure or mat, stood on edge until dry, and then used as bricks to build walls. Tough, durable walls result from these bricks (Fig. 1.6).

The use of bricks in more complex forms also must presume preplanning and some standard of measurement, perhaps the builder's own measuring stick or "rule". Egyptian examples from 2500 B.C. show a high degree of sophistication. Surviving measurement tools and surveying, engineering techniques substantiate this. Wall murals show production techniques of adobe bricks (Fig. 1.7), and biblical references indicate a specialization of tasks, where the Jews were assigned the task of making bricks. The use of straw and the responsibility for its supply are noted in Exodus 5:7.

In the Middle East, milleniums of civilization and population pressures created new demands for land and settlements in harsher arid environments.

FIGURE 1.6. **Cut sod bricks, Corrales, New Mexico, 1982. These are called *Terrones* in New Mexico, and may be identified by their squarish shape and integral root structure. Bruce McHenry photo.**

FIGURE 1.7. **Egyptian wall mural of adobe making. From the tomb of Queen Hatshepsut. Courtesy *Architecture for the Poor*, Hassan Fathy.**

FIGURE 1.8. **Iranian village, 1972. This village is constructed almost entirely of mud brick, in the form of arches, domes and vaults. Large building at the upper left has been in continuous use since 400 B.C.**

FIGURE 1.9. **Taos Pueblo, New Mexico, 1947 (built ca. 1000 A.D.). A multistoried community dwelling, still occupied and little changed since the Spanish Conquest in the 16th Century. The tribal leaders still refuse to allow the installation of electric service.**

Techniques were developed that required no structural members at all, and buildings were built entirely of mud brick (Fig. 1.8). The masonry vaulted forms, presumably developed in the Middle East prior to the Egyptian Dynastic Period, spread to North Africa and then to Roman cities. Later, Moorish invasions of Spain spread the use of these forms there. In turn, they were exported to the Western Hemisphere by Spanish explorers.

In the Spanish Southwest explorers found mud villages in 1540 (Fig. 1.9). Settlers from as early as 1590 brought adobe technology from the South, into an area with a long history of earth construction. Their use of adobe brick, not known to the Pueblo Indians except in rudimentary forms, was to set the standard for several centuries. The economic and transportation systems of the time made the use of locally available materials mandatory. The rapid westward expansion of the United States made wide use of this material, not only in the arid Southwest, but in nearly all of the western states. Local building suppliers provided "bricks" for sale, along with lumber and quicklime, all produced locally. In general, the settlers followed the local custom and tradition using rocks, logs, and mud, depending on the local conditions.

On the Eastern Seaboard, in many locations including South Carolina, New York, and Washington, D.C., rammed earth was used into the mid 19th century (Fig. 1.10). A treatise was published in 1839 extolling the virtues of rammed earth construction.[1] It is a viable medium in virtually any climate and does not require the curing time without rain necessary for the making of adobe bricks.

With the advent of the railroads pushing West in the 1880s, manufactured materials previously unavailable were in abundant supply. Then, as now, homeowners, builders, and merchants strived to upgrade building materials and emulate the styles of the East. As this pressure increased, the use of adobe bricks gradually declined. In spite of this trend, the use of adobe in rural situations, and for economy in many commercial buildings, still persisted. The great depression of the 1930s brought a rediscovery of the econ-

FIGURE 1.10. **The Church of The Holy Cross, Sumter, South Carolina, 1974 (ca. 1850). This church is built of rammed earth and is still in use today. Some modern repairs include concrete and modern masonry. Photo courtesy David and Lydia Miller, Rammed Earth Institute International, Greeley, Colorado.**

[7]

FIGURE 1.11. **Rabbit and poultry building State Fair Grounds, Albuquerque, New Mexico, 1982 (ca. 1930s). Many public buildings were built of adobe in New Mexico as late as World War II.**

omy of this material, and sparked a short-term interest with some of the oil companies who sponsored research and product development in stabilized (waterproof) adobes. Asphalt emulsion was used as a stabilizing agent. This effort seems to have been abandoned by the oil companies in the later 1940s.

A number of public buildings were built during the 1930s, and at least one school was built of adobe in New Mexico as late as 1940. Some architectural styles were in the traditional southwestern Pueblo or Territorial style, but many were of conventional styles, where the adobe brick was merely another type of common brick that was economical and available (Fig. 1.11).

In the decades since 1940 and World War II, our devotion to more modern materials led to a decline in the use of earth for building. Most construction in this medium was limited to either residential construction of large luxury homes where the owner could afford to indulge the nostalgia of Spanish Colonial styles, or to the very poor who had no other choice and were limited to what they could produce with their own hands. Thus, a split image was created, that adobe was for either the very rich or for the very poor, with little acceptance in between.

In the relative absence from the scene for a whole generation of architects, engineers, building officials, and builders using earth construction, the expertise became lost.

Changing economic conditions and energy shortages must lead us to a new evaluation of this historic material. Where as recently as 20 years ago adobe construction was dismissed as impractical or undesirable, because of the image of use by the very rich or the very poor, it is now being taken seriously and accepted as a logical building medium. It must again assume its place as an important, energy efficient building material.

**REFERENCE**    1. E. Gilman, *The Economical Builder*, J. Gideon, Washington, D.C., 1839.

*chapter two*
# Examples of Earth Architecture

Earth architecture can be found almost anywhere, but in our rush to make use of modern building methods, we have forgotten that it is still with us. Examples range from simple mud shelters to magnificent palaces. Earth for building is always beneath our feet, and in time of economic distress, we can always turn to Mother Earth for shelter.

The following photographs attempt to present the range and scope of earth architecture on a world-wide scale, from modest shelter to monumental efforts, historically and at the present time. In these photographs, it is difficult to determine the basic core of the building, as it is often sheathed with more durable stone or stucco. If they seem to represent poverty or neglect, it is unintentional, but mainly to show the underlying fabric.

It is possible here to show only the tip of the iceberg. Look around you and you will find earth buildings where you least expect them.

**WESTERN UNITED STATES**

Earth construction was used by the prehistoric peoples, the Spanish conquistadors and early pioneers throughout the West. It is still used today and is experiencing new popularity, partly by owner builders who use it for economy and forgiving technology, and partly by architects, builders, and artists who create live-in sculptures for more luxurious homes. It had wide popularity in rural areas, even for schools, churches, and public buildings until World War II. The adobe brick mode is the most popular in the West today, but many proponents of rammed earth are also building in this medium.

FIGURE 2.1. **Site 48, Santa Rosa, New Mexico, 1980 (ca. 1780–1820). A fortified *Comanchero* village built of adobe on the Pecos River. Photo courtesy Center for Anthropological Studies, Albuquerque, New Mexico.**

FIGURE 2.2. **McHenry house, Placitas, New Mexico, 1962. A traditional territorial style adobe home. Fired brick coping at the top of the parapet wall exemplifies this style. P. G. McHenry, Jr., Architect-Builder.**

FIGURE 2.3. **McHenry house continued. The hilltop site commands large vistas.**

FIGURE 2.4. **McHenry house, continued. Modern materials echo early territorial styles with beamed ceilings, brick floor, and colonial trim.**

FIGURE 2.5. **Tumacacori National Monument, USDI National Park Service. Tumacacori, Arizona, 1971 (ca. 1820). A mission church with massive (6 ft) adobe walls. Much of the ornate masonry decoration was built of fired adobe brick.**

FIGURE 2.6. **Tumacacori National Monument, continued. The visitor center was built of adobe in the 1930s in the original mission style.**

FIGURE 2.7. **Calvert house, Albuquerque, New Mexico, 1979. A passive solar adobe home in the Pueblo style. P. G. McHenry, Jr., Architect-Builder.**

FIGURE 2.8. **Calvert house, continued. Portions of the adobe brick walls were left unplastered to expose the massive brick texture.**

FIGURE 2.9. **Calvert house, continued. Varied textures of smooth plaster, exposed brick, rough sawn timbers and fine finished woodwork blend smoothly to create a pleasing contrast.**

FIGURE 2.10. **Calvert house, continued. Sculptural plaster forms a showcase setting for paintings and art works.**

FIGURE 2.11. **Palace of the Governor, Santa Fe, New Mexico, 1981 (ca. 1610). The massive walls of this early building were built in the local Indian style, as the seat of government for New Mexico, and is now a museum. Alterations during the Victorian era reflected the styles of the time, which were changed back to the "Santa Fe" or "Pueblo" style in the 1920s.**

FIGURE 2.12. **Casa de Armijo, Albuquerque, New Mexico, 1980 (ca. 1700). This rambling adobe home of Manuel Armijo, one of the early governors, on the Old Town Plaza reflects changing styles and available materials with the pitched tin roof. Changing economic needs now make use of this old home for a restaurant and shops.**

FIGURE 2.13. **Church, Pinos Altos, New Mexico, 1972 (ca. 1900). This church was built of adobes made on site in this mountain mining community. Rock foundations support adobe walls laid up with lime/sand mortar, perhaps reflecting a distrust of mud mortar by the builder.**

FIGURE 2.14. **Apartment house, Albuquerque, New Mexico, 1981 (ca. 1910). Victorian style with straight walls obscures the softer lines of most adobe buildings.**

FIGURE 2.15. **Warehouse, Gallup, New Mexico, 1980 (ca. 1915). The stout unplastered adobe walls of this warehouse still serve their original purpose in spite of railroad vibration nearby.**

FIGURE 2.16. **New Mexico State Fair Buildings, Albuquerque, New Mexico, 1982 (ca. 1930s). Adobe bricks for all types of buildings were economical and appropriate for public buildings.**

FIGURE 2.17. **St. Phillip's in the Hills, Tucson, Arizona, 1971 (ca. 1930s). Built basically of fired adobe bricks with ornate Baroque mission style detailing. This church still serves its congregation.**

[15]

FIGURE 2.18. Lister house, Corrales, New Mexico, 1971. This valley home incorporates several historical styles blending well with its natural setting. George Clayton Pearl, Architect; P. G. McHenry, Jr., Builder.

FIGURE 2.19. Lister house, continued. Soft adobe lines provide an opportunity for live-in sculptural forms with great charm.

FIGURE 2.20. **Miller house, Greeley, Colorado, 1950. This modern home is built of rammed earth, reflecting the architectural styles of the 1950s. Photo courtesy Lydia and David Miller, Rammed Earth Institute International, Greeley, Colorado.**

FIGURE 2.21. **Duday House, St. David., Arizona, 1977. Contemporary style was accomplished with rammed earth. Designed and built by Schmidt Builders, St. David, Arizona.**

FIGURE 2.22. **Walker House, Bisbee, Arizona, 1981. This passive solar rammed earth home, with wide overhangs for shade sits quietly in a desert setting. Brian Lockhart, Architect; Earth and Sun Construction, St. David, Arizona, Builders.**

FIGURE 2.23. **Bank of Cochise, Sierra Vista, Arizona, 1982. This modern bank building is built of rammed earth. Local building codes required reinforced concrete structural members. Schuman Wilson Associates, Tucson, Arizona, Architects; Schmidt Builders, Earth and Sun Construction St. David, Arizona.**

[ **17** ]

FIGURE 2.24. **Minge house, Corrales, New Mexico, 1979. A magnificent example of restorations and new additions, using salvaged historic building elements. A rambling house surrounds the *Plasuela* garden in a traditional pattern. Alan Minge, Historian-Restorer.**

FIGURE 2.25. **Minge house, continued. Traditional *horno* corner fireplaces are found in nearly every room. It is more of a masonry hood for a corner firepit than a conventional fireplace. A simple form, it is easily built and provides a great amount of heat. Darker painted wainscote hides soil, and white upper walls reflect available light, providing a setting for antique *retablos*. Painted pottery decorative forms are appropriate.**

FIGURE 2.26. **Fox house, Albuquerque, New Mexico, 1964.** The entrance to this adobe home is secured with a walled forecourt and strong barred portals, reminiscent of early dwellings. P. G. McHenry, Jr., Architect-Builder.

FIGURE 2.27. **Grisham house, Albuquerque, New Mexico, 1978.** This passive solar home has large expanses of glass on the southern exposure, with overhangs to block sun entry in the summer. A garden wall of asphalt-stabilized adobes shields the entrance, and supplies a warm, wind-free space for flower gardens. P. G. McHenry, Jr., Architect-Builder.

FIGURE 2.28. **Ratcliff house, Los Ranchos de Albuquerque, New Mexico, 1979.** The addition of clearstory windows added light and solar gain to a darker north room. Original exposed vigas and sculptured adobe walls provide intricate shadow patterns from the sunlight above. P. G. McHenry, Jr., Architect-Builder.

[19]

FIGURE 2.29. **Rogers house, Albuquerque, New Mexico, 1971. Simple but elegant Pueblo Style is highlighted with Territorial Style window pediments. John Gaw Meen, Architect.**

FIGURE 2.30. **The Fort restaurant, Denver, Colorado, 1981. A modern restaurant was built of adobe to the plan of Bent's Old Fort, a trading point on the Santa Fe Trail in the 1830s. Modern amenities are cleverly hidden behind soft lines. Photo courtesy W. E. Meyer, Western Energy Planners, Aurora, Colorado.**

FIGURE 2.31. **Branch house, Albuquerque, New Mexico, 1982 (1964). Thick adobe walls provide an island of quiet on a small city lot near a busy street. P. G. McHenry, Jr., Architect-Builder.**

FIGURE 2.32. **Larabee house, Albuquerque, New Mexico, 1982 (1964). A low profile follows a gently sloping site sinking this adobe house into its surroundings. Mature landscaping shades the thick walls in summer. P. G. McHenry, Jr., Architect-Builder.**

FIGURE 2.33. **Schmidt house, Albuquerque, New Mexico, 1982 (1961). The elegance of this formal Territorial style is complimented by the earth colored stucco walls. P. G. McHenry, Jr., Architect-Builder.**

[21]

FIGURE 2.34. **Schmidt house, continued. Cool porches, stark white trim are accented by hand-crafted wrought iron light fixtures.**

FIGURE 2.35. **Schmidt house, continued. Large windows were seldom used in historic adobe homes for reasons of security and cost. Modern standards dictate larger windows for light, ventilation, and solar gain. New bricks were aged by tumbling in a cement mixer.**

FIGURE 2.36. **Schmidt house, continued. Hand-painted tile accents used sparingly, and fine wood surfaces help create a rich visual flavor. Floor tiles are hydraulically pressed colored concrete.**

FIGURE 2.37. **Dar Al Islam Mosque, Abiquiu, New Mexico, 1982. A religious group adopted Middle Eastern architectural styles for their mosque, using locally made adobe bricks. Little wood was required, using masonry arches, domes, and barrel vaults for roof structures. Hassan Fathy, Architect.**

FIGURE 2.38. **Dar Al Islam Mosque, continued. Skilled masonry crews from Egypt build massive adobe arches, training local masons for future work.**

FIGURE 2.39. **Dar Al Islam, continued.** Large lightweight plywood forms support arch masonry until the key bricks are in place. An interpreter translates instructions from Egyptian to English.

FIGURE 2.40. **McHenry house, Corrales, New Mexico, 1981 (1976).** Super thick (20 in.) adobe brick walls rest on gravel foundations, without concrete or reinforcing steel. An adobe brick dome and barrel vault are used for part of the roof structure. P. G. McHenry, Jr., Architect-Builder.

FIGURE 2.41. **McHenry house, continued.** Skylights and indoor planters relate interior spaces to outside greenery in a rural setting. Hallway is wide enough to furnish, giving a generous feeling of space.

FIGURE 2.42. **McHenry house, continued. Entry hall is roofed with an adobe brick barrel vault. Colorful stained glass and white walls offer a pleasing contrast.**

FIGURE 2.43. **McHenry house, continued. Corner fireplaces are functional for heating as well as sculptural decoration. Ceiling-high fixed glass panels bring the outdoors in and visually enlarge the space.**

FIGURE 2.44. **McHenry house, continued. Thick walls are accentuated at the window jambs. Wide brick sills are ideal for plants and decoration.**

FIGURE 2.45. **McHenry house, continued. Functional fireplaces in bedrooms add charm. Wall at left is plastered frame to accommodate plumbing stacks.**

[26]

FIGURE 2.46. **McHenry house, continued. Adobe brick walls are plastered with adobe soil made from unscreened material, giving an uneven texture. Final finish was floated with a wet sheepskin, sealed, and painted with flat latex. Ceiling timbers and deck are stained with a colored clay soil and water mix.**

FIGURE 2.47. **McHenry house, continued. Design of wall forms and shapes can be flexible with adobe masonry. The small door on the right was just for fun.**

FIGURE 2.48. **Olson house, Albuquerque, New Mexico, 1978.** A splashing fountain of hand-carved volcanic stone, highlighted with a Mexican tile background, adds a cool feeling to this garden room. Bronze anodized aluminum windows were specified for economy, but do not clash with the other decor. P. G. McHenry, Jr., Architect-Builder.

FIGURE 2.49. **Miller house, Albuquerque, New Mexico, 1978.** This solar adobe home grows out of its rugged mountain site, echoing colors and textures of the landscape. Site boulders and vegetation were carefully protected during construction. P. G. McHenry, Jr., Architect-Builder.

[28]

FIGURE 2.50. **Miller house, continued. A massive adobe structure serves several functions, as supporting structure and as room divider with built-in seating, and two fireplaces.**

FIGURE 2.51. **La Luz, Albuquerque, New Mexico, 1982 (1970). A large townhouse complex was built on a suburban site, with magnificent vistas of the nearby mountains. Bruce McHenry photo. Antoine Predock, Architect.**

FIGURE 2.52. **La Luz, Albuquerque, New Mexico, 1982. A sense of privacy is insured by careful orientation and garden walls of individual units. Heavy adobe common walls between units have virtually no sound transmission. Bruce McHenry photo.**

**EASTERN UNITED STATES**

While the buildings of the eastern United States might seem more logically suited to more traditional wood, fired brick, stone, and concrete, many of the early buildings were of earth. The damper climate limited the use of adobe bricks and made the use of rammed earth more feasible. Plantations of the South, private homes in Washington, D.C., churches, and public buildings made use of this medium as well, although few examples remain. The few examples shown here are among the survivors, although there are many more. The U.S. Department of Agriculture sponsored research and built experimental buildings to demonstrate the feasibility during the depression of the 1930s. The advent of World War II and the boom times that followed led to a decrease in efforts and research in this field.

FIGURE 2.53. **Church of The Holy Cross, Sumter, South Carolina, 1974 (ca. 1850). This church was originally built of rammed earth and has withstood earthquake and hurricane. More recent repairs have been with concrete. Photo courtesy Lydia and David Miller, Rammed Earth Institute International, Greeley, Colorado.**

FIGURE 2.54. **An adobe brick house, Rochester, New York, 1981 (ca. 1835). These bricks were made from clay from a nearby creek, and the building is now being renovated to a modern home by a university professor and his wife. Photo courtesy Gary Lehman, Rochester, New York.**

FIGURE 2.55. A demonstration home, Gardendale, Alabama, ca. 1935. This rammed earth home was built by the U.S. Department of Agriculture as a demonstration. Photo courtesy Lydia and David Miller, Rammed Earth Institute International, Greeley, Colorado. A number of similar projects were also done in western states with adobe bricks during the great depression of the 1930s, and are still in use today.

These regions were mainly explored and settled by people from Spain and Portugal, who brought new forms to existing earth construction tradition. There was some use of mud brick and other forms of earth construction by pre-Columbian peoples. European explorers and settlers brought new dimensions in an echo of more monumental forms from home, and imposed some surprising examples on the local scene. Current governmental policy trends still favor more modern materials and tend to equate earth materials with poverty. Increasing needs, and rising energy costs must bring about a re-evaluation of these policies.

## MEXICO AND LATIN AMERICA

FIGURE 2.56. Hacienda San Diego ranch headquarters, Chihuahua, Mexico, 1979 (ca. 1915). This large ranch building was built by Luis Terrazas, a Mexican cattle baron, before the revolution. It is one of 19 similar ranch headquarters of his in this state. Carved stone, fired brick, and wrought iron offer an Italianate motif.

FIGURE 2.57. **Casas Grandes ruin, Casas Grandes, Chihuahua, Mexico, 1978 (ca. 900 A.D.). This large multistory prehistoric settlement was built entirely of puddled mud incorporating some sophisticated refinements referred to in other chapters.**

FIGURE 2.58. **The Playa de Cortez Hotel, Guaymas, Sonora, Mexico, 1971 (ca. 1930s). This large adobe complex is the ultimate in the monumental Mexican style.**

FIGURE 2.59. **Town plaza, Magdalena, Sonora, Mexico, 1971 (ca. 1978). Traditional Spanish Colonial styles, blended with an earlier Aztec motif is striking.**

FIGURE 2.60. **Plaza shopping center, Magdalena, Sonora, Mexico.** Modern amenities are well hidden behind the traditional facade.

FIGURE 2.61. **Iglesia de Santa Ana, Chipaya, Bolivia, 1979 (ca. 1830).** This tall, adobe church tower is butressed at the corners, either as a repair or in the original. Photos courtesy (Arq.) Teresa Gisbert, La Paz, Bolivia.

FIGURE 2.62. **The Village of Santa Ana, Chipaya, Bolivia, 1979.** Thatched roofs indicate a quantity of small vegetation is close by, perhaps from a lake or marshy area.

FIGURE 2.63. **Rural Homes, Chapaya, Bolivia, 1979.** These rural dwellings use a corbelled brick roof structure totally different from the village homes, for reasons unknown. Both are circular in form, but with different roof structures.

[33]

FIGURE 2.64. **Rua S. Pedro, Lencois, Bahia, Brazil, 1972. Stone, adobe brick, and jacal (exposed by plaster peeling on the right) are all side by side in this village. Photos courtesy Augosto C. Da Silva Telles, Director, Patrimonio Historico E Artistico Nacional, Rio de Janiero, Brazil.**

FIGURE 2.65. **Palacete Palmiera, Pindamonhangaba, SP, Brazil (ca. 1850). External walls of *taipa de pilao* (jacal?) protected with stucco. Highly ornamental forms such as this frequently conceal the simple structure.**

FIGURE 2.66. **Antiga Casa de Camara e Cadeia, Goias, Velho, Brazil, 1949 (ca. 1776). Walls of adobe brick and *taipa de pilao*.**

Architectural tradition in Europe is most often thought of in Gothic, **EUROPE**
Beaux Art, or Modern styles, but in many rural areas, earth construction has
been widely used for many centuries. France has an ongoing tradition of
rammed earth (Pise'), Germany has extant examples of monumental buildings of great age, and even England with its damp, humid climate has some.

FIGURE 2.67. **Rammed earth (Pise') Chateau, Dolomieux, France. Photo courtesy Centre de Documentation Photographique sur l'architecture. Photographies de Christin Bastin et Jacques Evrard, 127 rue de l'Arbre Benit, 1050 Brussels, Belgium.**

FIGURE 2.68. **House of Earth Hotel, Macon, France, 1949 (ca. 1790). A three-story building of rammed earth, serving well after almost three centuries. Photo courtesy of Lydia and David Miller, Rammed Earth Institute International, Greeley, Colorado.**

FIGURE 2.69. **Rammed earth (*Pise'*) Chateau, Dolomieux, France. The exterior stucco is in need of repair. Photo courtesy of Centre de Documentation Photographique sur l'Architecture. Photographies de Christin Bastin et Jacques Evrard, 127 rue de l'Arbre Benit 1050 Brussels, Belgium.**

FIGURE 2.70. **Barn of earth, Bokrijk, Belgium. This earth building appears to be of post and beam frame, with earth infill panels. Photo courtesy Centre de Documentation Photographique sur l'Architecture. Photographies de Christin Bastin et Jacques Evrard, 127 rue de l'Arbre Benit, 1950, Brussels, Belgium.**

FIGURE 2.71. **Sleeping Beauty Castle, Weilburg, Germany, 1949. This monumental structure is of rammed earth. Photo courtesy Lydia and David Miller, Rammed Earth Institute International, Greeley, Colorado.**

FIGURE 2.72. **Store and apartment building, Weilburg, Germany, 1949 (ca. 1820). This wood-reinforced earth building is three stories high, and underwent major repairs within the past 50 years. Photo courtesy Lydia and David Miller, Rammed Earth Institute International, Greeley, Colorado.**

FIGURE 2.73. **A six-story apartment house, Weilburg, Germany, 1949. This hillside site requires three storys on one side and six storys on the other, built of rammed earth. Photo courtesy Lydia and David Miller, Rammed Earth Institute, Greeley, Colorado.**

FIGURE 2.74. **Phicardou Village, Troodos Mountains, Cyprus. A combination of stone and adobe bricks are used here, the stone mainly for the lower floors and the bottom of the walls. Photo(s) courtesy Demos Christou and Androulla Floridou, Ministry of Communications and Works, Department of Antiquities, Nicosia, Cyprus.**

[ **37** ]

FIGURE 2.75. **Kakopetria Village, Troodos Mountains, Cyprus. A home of stone and adobe brick after restoration.**

FIGURE 2.76. **Kakopetria Village, continued. All stone masons have a distinct technique that is like a signature. Several masons have worked on these walls. Upper floor is of adobe brick, plastered smoothly with straw reinforced mud plaster.**

FIGURE 2.77. **Townhouse, Nicosia, Cyprus. Adobe bricks and mud plaster are finally coated with** *asbestis* **(lime?) whitewash for clean color.**

FIGURE 2.78. **Folk-architecture home, Mesaoria Valley, Cyprus. The protruding roof timbers and "beehive" oven are also common to the southwestern United States. This photograph could represent many scenes in New Mexico. Foundations are also of adobe brick.**

**AFRICA**   Developing nations in rural Africa use earth building techniques, some of which are very simple and have remained unchanged for millenia, for dwellings and grain storage buildings. Many other configurations of mud-brick building techniques employ sophisticated architectural forms.

FIGURE 2.79. **Oasis Kharga, Egypt. This large building is roofed with a series of barrel vaults. The vault thickness is approximately 10 in. (25 cm). Adobe bricks are also used for the latticework closing the vault ends, providing light and ventilation. Photo courtesy Centre de Documentation Photographiques sur l'Architecture. Photographies de Christin Bastin et Jacques Evrard, 127 rue de l'Abre Benit, 1050 Brussels Belgium. Hassan Fathy-Architect.**

FIGURE 2.80. **Gharb, Aswan, Egypt. Adobe brick walls are yet uncovered with plaster, exposing the sound masonry coursing pattern of two courses flat and one course on edge as a bonding course. Mud brick domes in the background are typical of much Islamic architecture. Photo courtesy Centre de Documentation Photographiques sur l'Architecture. Photographies de Christin Bastin et Jacques Evrard, 127 rue de l'Abre Benit, 1050 Brussels, Belgium.**

FIGURE 2.81. **Luxor, Egypt. Photo courtesy Centre de Documentation Photographiques sur l'Architecture. Photographies de Christin Bastin et Jacques Evrard, 127 rue de l'Abre Benit, 1050 Brussels, Belgium.**

FIGURE 2.82. **Luxor, Egypt. This photo details the square bottom shape, corner bridging squinch arches, and transition to a herringbone-patterned adobe brick dome. Photo courtesy Centre de Documentation Photographiques sur l'Architecture. Photographies de Christin Bastin et Jacques Evrard, 127 rue de l'Abre Benit, 1050 Brussels, Belgium.**

FIGURE 2.83. **El Maadher, Algeria. Rooftop shows intricate pattern of domes and barrel vaults. It appears that the surfaces have been covered with a thin coating of cement. Photo courtesy Centre de Documentation Photographiques sur l'Architecture. Photographies de Christin Bastin et Jacques Evrard, 127 rue de l'Abre Benit, 1050 Brussels, Belgium.**

[41]

FIGURE 2.84. **Rural village, Upper Volta, Africa. Sculptural shapes and mud plaster are a form of folk art that are distinctive. Photo courtesy Centre de Documentation Photographiques sur l'Architecture. Photographies de Christin Bastin et Jacques Evrard, 127 rue de l'Abre Benit, 1050 Brussels, Belgium.**

FIGURE 2.85. **Rural village, Upper Volta, Africa. These mud brick, domed roofs are a change from the thatched roofs of the dwellings in the background. That, coupled with the fact that they are raised off the ground, may indicate that they are grain-storage structures. Photo courtesy Centre de Documentation Photographiques sur l'Architecture. Photographies de Christin Bastin et Jacques Evrard, 127 rue de l'Abre Benit, 1050 Brussels, Belgium.**

FIGURE 2.86. **Village mosque, Upper Volta, Africa. This form, with a high central tower and enclosing courtyard, indicate that this is a mosque. Most of the earth construction is in a puddled form, not as strong as adobe bricks, requiring the supporting pilasters for the height. The wood members extending from the tower are a permanent form of scaffolding. Photo courtesy Centre de Documentation Photographiques sur l'Architecture. Photographies de Christin Bastin et Jacques Evrard, 127 rue de l'Abre Benit, 1050 Brussels, Belgium.**

The Middle East, which has some of the most hostile environments in the world, has spent thousands of years developing architectural forms employing mud brick. Lacking a supply of structural wood members, the ingenuity of the builders and architects was taxed to the utmost to create roof structures from small bricks. These vaulted forms have been found as early as 8000 B.C. Many of these exquisite forms have been forsaken for concrete or steel.

**THE MIDDLE EAST**

FIGURE 2.87. **Queen's Palace, Lashkar, Gah, Afghanistan, 1971 (ca. 1000 A.D.). Photo courtesy of Rebecca Shankland, Los Alamos, New Mexico.**

FIGURE 2.88. **Mosque of Nine Domes, Balkh, Afghanistan, 1971. Rough adobe masonry in the background is the basic fabric for this building. Plaster provides the final finish to cover the coarse work. Photo courtesy Rebecca Shankland, Los Alamos, New Mexico.**

[43]

FIGURE 2.89. **Mosque of Nine Domes, continued. Incised plaster decoration. The type of plaster used is not known, but is very likely made up of gypsum. Intricate plaster decoration is an art form that is becoming lost in the Middle East. Photo courtesy Rebecca Shankland, Los Alamos, New Mexico.**

FIGURE 2.90. **Village view, Say'un, South Yemen. This entire village is made up of multistory earth buildings in a desert setting. Photo courtesy Centre de Documentation Photographiques sur l'Architecture. Photographies de Christin Bastin et Jacques Evrard, 127 rue de l'Abre Benit, 1050 Brussels, Belgium.**

FIGURE 2.91. **Ancient Palace, Tarim, South Yemen. This intricate facade is covered with a wash-plaster coating, which has been stained by adobe dirt washing down across it. Photo courtesy Centre de Documentation Photographiques sur l'Architecture. Photographies de Christin Bastin et Jacques Evrard, 127 rue de l'Abre Benit, 1050 Brussels, Belgium.**

FIGURE 2.92. **Village School, Faraj, Iran, 1972 (ca. 400 B.C.). This strong, former fortress has been continually occupied for more than two millenia. Indented crenelations were for bow and arrow defense. Main walls are of adobe brick, but low yard wall is of puddled mud (Chine).**

FIGURE 2.93. **The Shah Abbas hotel, Isfahan, Iran, 1972. This old *caravanserie* was converted to a luxury hotel in the 1920s. Precise landscaping, reflective pools, and colorful tile decoration in the central courtyard are of breathtaking beauty. A portion of it was burned during the Ayatolla Khomeni's revolution.**

FIGURE 2.94. **Bazaar roof, Isfahan, Iran, 1972.** The entire roof of the main bazaar, one of the world's largest, is roofed entirely with mud. Domed and vaulted structures are given light and ventilation with the glass cupolas on top. In spite of a heavy rain the day before, little evidence of roof damage could be seen.

FIGURE 2.95. **Fortified village, southern Iran, 1972 (ca. 1500 B.C.).** The primary maintenance problem with adobe walls is basal coving, seen clearly here. Wall repairs have been made with adobe bricks. Roofing in this locale is done with thatch and mud, rather than vaulted brick forms found in more arid regions of Iran.

FIGURE 2.96. **Desert ice plant (*Kah*), central Iran.** Water in flooded ponds on the north side of the 40-ft high walls is frozen at night, cut, and stored underground in the domed structure to the right. Patterned masonry decorates the high walls to the left.

## chapter three

# Soil Selection

Soil for the making of adobe bricks or for use in rammed earth walls is available in virtually unlimited quantities almost everywhere. Obviously, some soils may be ideal, and some unsuitable, but most will be satisfactory with only minor modifications. A common misconception is that the soil must be a special "adobe" soil. Examples of earth-wall structures can be found from high mountain passes to the humid lowlands of the Eastern seaboard.

**OCCURRENCE**

Soil maps, as generally presented, have limited value in the selection of a soil source for earth construction. Standard soil maps classify the soils geologically in several broad categories and further identify them somewhat as to mineral makeup, age, and geologic source. Most soils are "old" or "young". In a relatively immature geologic area, such as the southwestern portion of the United States, most of the geologic soil formations are young, and other areas such as the river drainage basins of the Midwest and East, are mature, or old. The older soils in mature geologic areas tend to be more complex chemically and physically, and generally clays in these formations are heavier. A high percentage of organic material may also be present. Geological maps may be more useful, and some simple soil maps may offer a limited amount of information. In an area long recognized for the use of adobe, such as the Rio Grande River Valley in New Mexico, many of the soils are relatively young. Most of the soil formations are alluvial fans, often connected to form a piedmont plain. These plains are made up of layers of soil and gravel deposits. Generally the topmost layer is very sandy, with a large proportion of windblown sand, the clays and silt having been leached by rain to a lower level. The clay layers can be recognized in arroyo banks and eroded channels where a cross section of underlying strata is exposed (Fig. 3.1). The clay layers so exposed will be relatively vertical in cross section of eroded areas and may be a different color than the overburden. Most of the soil orders found in the Rio Grande Valley are classified as Aridisols and Entisols. The Entisols lie primarily in the valleys and the Aridisols as higher plateaus, suitable mostly for grazing. The other orders, Molisols, Inceptisols, and Alfisols can be and are also used for adobe bricks. The workable tolerance for coarser gravels and variation in particle size is broad, despite some building code requirements limiting particle size.

Soil is heavy, and to minimize transportation costs, the source is best located close to, if not directly on the building site. Often surplus soil from excavation of basements, cesspools, or major grading changes can be utilized for the manufacture of bricks or mortar. The best practical test for determining the suitability of a soil for bricks is to make several sample bricks from the soil source most economically viable to the building site or manufacturing yard. Due to the weight of soil, the transportation cost of the material will increase rapidly between source, manufacturing point, and point of use.

Simple field soil tests can be made with a glass jar and water. The jar is partially filled with the proposed soil, and water is added to a distance above the soil level. The mixture is shaken and allowed to settle until the water becomes clear. The resulting bands of coarser aggregates at the bottom, sand, silt, and clay on top will indicate the approximate proportions of various ingredients (Fig. 3.2a,b).

Additional simple field testing for clay content and plasticity can be done with the *rope* test. A sample of the soil is mixed with a small amount of water to make a stiff lump of mud. The mud is rolled by hand into a ropelike shape (Fig. 3.2c). The plasticity of the soil rope and its cracking upon drying will indicate the clay content. Drying cracks indicate an excess of clay.

**CHARACTERISTICS**     Ideally, for use in earth wall construction, the soil must contain four elements: coarse sand or aggregate, fine sand, silt, and clay. Any one may be totally absent and the soil may still make satisfactory bricks. The various elements may be likened to the ingredients of concrete: aggregate, sand, and cement. The coarse sand or aggregate represents the aggregate, the fine sand for the sand, and the silt and clay for the cement. The aggregate (sand) provides strength, the fine sand is a filler to lock the grains of aggregate, and the silt and clay (generally identified by particle size rather than chemical analysis) act as a binder and plastic medium to glue the other ingredients together. Soil structures with a high percentage of aggregate (sand) may be strong when dry, but are more vulnerable to erosion from rain. Soil structures high in clay may be much more resistant to water and erosion, but less strong.

FIGURE 3.1. (*a*) Typical adobe soil sources, Corrales, New Mexico. Erosion caused the exposure of underlying soil strata. The high-clay material is seen near the top with a steep vertical surface. The topmost layer is sandy loam, or "blow sand" which may have fine particles worn to a round shape as compared to "sharp" sand which is better for construction. Adobe soil is also found in river bottom land, which is frequently high in clay. (*b*) Adobe soil source, Salida, Colorado, 1981. This material would appear to have too many stones for the production of adobe bricks. Tests on bricks made from this material tested to higher quality than many of those made from other sources that looked more promising.

FIGURE 3.2. Jar test for soil. (*a*) A handful of soil shaken in a jar with water will indicate composition, with larger, heavier elements settling first at the bottom. (*b*) After settling, which may take 24 hours or more, gradations and proportions of material may be seen. The clay, normally of a lighter color, will be at the top. (*c*) Rope test. This is done by adding enough water to a handful of adobe soil to make a moldable plastic "rope" which will indicate the plasticity and clay content. Bruce McHenry photos.

[**49**]

**PROPORTIONS**    Bank run soils, as they naturally occur, may vary widely in proportions of aggregate, sand, silt, and clay, and the brick maker must be prepared to modify the material as it is processed.

Tests of soils and the resultant bricks made from them have been conducted by a number of organizations. One of the most significant series of tests was done by the U.S. Department of Interior, National Park Service, in which soil samples from a wide range of successful adobe structures of great age were examined for particle size, clay content, and type. Tables 3.1, 3.2, 3.3, and 3.4 indicate the wide range found, leading to the conclusion that the proportional tolerance is extremely wide. Many naturally occurring soils will require some modification, more often to deal with the presence of too much clay, rather than the lack of it. The soil abundant in clay may be modified by the addition of sand, coarser aggregates, or vegetal matter such as straw, hay, or manure. It is perhaps unrealistic to try to establish rigid proportions in view of the nature of the material sources and the lack of difference in the performance of the finished product. If an ideal proportion were to be established, it might represent an average of samples taken from successful structures. Using Tables 3.1, 3.2, and 3.3, this would yield the following:

TABLE 3.1

**Soil Material Composition for Adobes, Mortar, and Mud Plaster—Average Percent of Total Sample**

| Location | Gravel | C Sand | F Sand | Silt | Clay | Porosity |
|---|---|---|---|---|---|---|
| Tumacacori, Arizona[a] | | | | | | |
| Adobes | | | | | | |
| P1  10 samples | 14.4 | 20.2 | 24.8 | 27.8 | 13.9 | 32.3 |
| P2   8 samples | 10.7 | 23.7 | 30.1 | 25.8 | 9.7 | 33.1 |
| P3  12 samples | 10.5 | 22.2 | 28.9 | 27.0 | 11.2 | 34.6 |
| P4   8 samples | 12.1 | 24.4 | 29.8 | 24.9 | 9.0 | 31.0 |
| P5  13 samples | 8.0 | 18.6 | 30.1 | 26.7 | 18.0 | 34.2 |
| P6  10 samples | 8.2 | 19.7 | 29.4 | 31.1 | 11.5 | — |
| Galisteo, New Mexico | | | | | | |
| Soil source | 6.0 | 10.0 | 43.0 | 34.0 | 7.0 | — |
| For bricks | 2.5 | 2.5 | 25.0 | 49.0 | 21.0 | — |
| Jemez Springs, New Mexico | | | | | | |
| Mud plaster | 5.0 | 6.0 | 51.0 | 26.0 | 12.0 | — |
| Mud plaster | 12.5 | 18.6 | 23.2 | 36.1 | 9.6 | — |
| Trampas, New Mexico | | | | | | |
| Mud plaster | 4.6 | 5.4 | 14.4 | 50.5 | 25.1 | — |
| Mud plaster | 10.6 | 21.0 | 23.1 | 28.3 | 17.0 | — |
| Quari, New Mexico | | | | | | |
| Mud plaster | 0.3 | 9.0 | 24.9 | 48.1 | 17.7 | — |
| Gunnison, Colorado | | | | | | |
| Interior mud plaster | 0. | 12.0 | 51.0 | 21.0 | 16.0 | — |
| Sasabe, Mexico | | | | | | |
| High clay added | | | | | | |
| for mixing | 1.9 | 23.1 | 28.9 | 16.3 | 29.8 | — |
| standard soil/bricks | 7.9 | 17.1 | 16.0 | 40.9 | 18.1 | — |
| Average | 7.2 | 15.8 | 29.6 | 32.1 | 15.4 | 33.0 |

[a] Tumacacori Mission built around 1820 A.D.

*Note:* Particle size AASHO Standard: Gravel, over 2.000 mm; C sand, 2.000–0.425 mm; F sand, 0.425–0.075 mm; silt, 0.075–0.005 mm; clay, less than 0.005 mm.

*Data Source:* USDI—National Park Service, Western Archaeology Center, Tucson, Arizona.

| | |
|---|---|
| Sand or coarse aggregate | 23% |
| Sand or fine sand | 30% |
| Silt | 32% |
| Clay | 15% |

The analysis of soils to determine quantities of silt and clay is more commonly done on a particle size basis, rather than by more accurate methods. It may be that these two ingredients are somewhat interchangeable. It has been observed, however, that although high silt soils with little clay may have some of the apparent physical characteristics of clay soil, they may not be as strong and will not be as water resistant.

TABLE 3.2
**Soil Material Composition for Adobes, Mortar, and Mud Plaster—High–Low Percent of Total Sample**

| Location | Gravel | | C Sand | | F Sand | | Silt | | Clay | |
|---|---|---|---|---|---|---|---|---|---|---|
| | High | Low | High | Low | High | Low | High | Low | High | Low |
| Tumacacori, Arizona | | | | | | | | | | |
| P1 | 37.0 | 6.0 | 29.0 | 11.0 | 35.0 | 16.0 | 39.0 | 14.0 | 17.0 | 9.0 |
| P2 | 30.0 | 4.0 | 30.0 | 16.5 | 45.0 | 20.0 | 43.0 | 10.0 | 17.0 | 1.0 |
| P3 | 25.0 | 2.0 | 26.5 | 14.0 | 40.5 | 18.0 | 39.0 | 19.0 | 25.0 | 5.0 |
| P4 | 26.0 | 3.0 | 34.0 | 20.0 | 39.0 | 22.0 | 35.0 | 17.0 | 14.0 | 5.0 |
| P5 | 19.0 | 1.0 | 23.0 | 15.0 | 41.5 | 19.0 | 41.0 | 20.0 | 24.0 | 11.0 |
| P6 | 21.8 | 4.4 | 28.0 | 11.3 | 44.2 | 23.4 | 40.9 | 16.2 | 18.7 | 7.1 |
| Average | 26.4 | 3.4 | 28.4 | 14.6 | 40.9 | 19.7 | 39.6 | 16.0 | 19.3 | 6.4 |

Conclusions: Soil composition varies widely with little effect. Averages from 71 samples; high–low from 61 samples.

| | | % | Note |
|---|---|---|---|
| Gravel | High | 26.4 | |
| | Low | 3.4 | |
| | Average | 7.2 | Lower percentage in plasters |
| C sand | High | 28.4 | |
| | Low | 14.6 | |
| | Average | 15.8 | |
| F Sand | High | 40.9 | |
| | Low | 19.7 | |
| | Average | 29.6 | |
| Silt | High | 39.6 | |
| | Low | 16.0 | |
| | Average | 32.1 | |
| Clay | High | 19.3 | |
| | Low | 6.4 | One sample (P2) with 1% clay indicated severe erosion. Slightly higher in plasters |

*Note:* Particle size AASHO Standard: Gravel, over 2.000 mm; C sand, 2.000–0.425 mm; F sand, 0.425–0.075 mm; silt, 0.075–0.005 mm; clay, less than 0.005 mm.
*Data Source:* USDI—National Park Service, Western Archaeology Center, Tucson, Arizona.

TABLE 3.3
**Soil Material Composition for Adobes, Mortar, and Mud Plaster—High–Low
Percent of Total Sample**

| | | Mont-moril-linite | Mica | Vermiculite | Chlorite | Kaolin | Int |
|---|---|---|---|---|---|---|---|
| Tumacacori, Arizona | | | | | | | |
| | P1 | 3 | 3 | 0 | 0 | 2 | 0 |
| | | 3 | 3 | 0 | 0 | 2 | 0 |
| | | 3 | 3 | 0 | 0 | 2 | 0 |
| | | 2 | 3 | 0 | 0 | 2 | 0 |
| | | 3 | 3 | 0 | 0 | 2 | 0 |
| | | 3 | 3 | 0 | 0 | 2 | 0 |
| | | 3 | 3 | 0 | 0 | 2 | 0 |
| | | 3 | 3 | 0 | 0 | 2 | 0 |
| | | 2 | 3 | 0 | 0 | 2 | 0 |
| | P2 | 1 | 4 | 0 | 0 | 2 | 0 |
| | | 1 | 4 | 0 | 0 | 2 | 0 |
| | | 1 | 4 | 0 | 0 | 2 | 0 |
| | | 1 | 3 | 0 | 0 | 1 | 0 |
| | | 1 | 4 | 0 | 0 | 2 | 0 |
| | | 0 | 2 | 0 | 1 | 1 | 0 |
| | | 1 | 3 | 4 | 0 | 0 | 2 |
| | P3 | 0 | 4 | 0 | 0 | 2 | 0 |
| | | 1 | 4 | 0 | 0 | 2 | 0 |
| | | 1 | 4 | 0 | 0 | 2 | 0 |
| | | 1 | 4 | 0 | 0 | 2 | 0 |
| | | 1 | 4 | 0 | 0 | 2 | 0 |
| | | 1 | 4 | 0 | 0 | 2 | 0 |
| | | 0 | 4 | 0 | 0 | 2 | 0 |
| | | 2 | 3 | 0 | 0 | 2 | 0 |
| | | 1 | 3 | 0 | 0 | 2 | 0 |
| | | 3 | 3 | 0 | 0 | 3 | 0 |
| | | 2 | 4 | 0 | 0 | 2 | 0 |
| | | 3 | 4 | 0 | 0 | 3 | 0 |
| | P4 | 1 | 3 | 0 | 0 | 2 | 0 |
| | | 1 | 4 | 0 | 0 | 3 | 0 |
| | | 1 | 4 | 0 | 0 | 2 | 0 |
| | | 1 | 4 | 0 | 0 | 2 | 0 |
| | | 2 | 4 | 0 | 0 | 2 | 0 |
| | | 1 | 4 | 0 | 0 | 2 | 0 |
| | | 2 | 4 | 0 | 0 | 2 | 0 |
| | P5 | 3 | 4 | 0 | 0 | 2 | 0 |
| | | 3 | 3 | 0 | 0 | 2 | 0 |
| | | 2 | 3 | 0 | 0 | 2 | 0 |
| | | 3 | 3 | 0 | 0 | 2 | 0 |
| | | 1 | 3 | 0 | 1 | 2 | 0 |
| | | 1 | 3 | 0 | 0 | 0 | 0 |
| | | 2 | 3 | 0 | 1 | 2 | 0 |
| | P6 | not tested | | | | | |
| Gallisteo, New Mexico | | 2 | 3 | 0 | 0 | 3 | 0 |
| | | 4 | 2 | 0 | 0 | 3 | 0 |
| Jemez Springs, New Mexico | | 4 | 2 | 0 | 0 | 3 | 0 |
| | | 0 | 3 | 1 | 1 | 3 | 0 |
| Trampas, New Mexico | | 5 | 2 | 0 | 0 | 1 | 0 |
| | | 2 | 2 | 0 | 0 | 2 | 0 |
| Quari, New Mexico | | 1 | 3 | 0 | 0 | 2 | 0 |
| Gunnison, Colorado | | 2 | 3 | 0 | 0 | 3 | 0 |
| Sasabe, Mexico | | not made | | | | | |

*Code:*  5, Dominant; 4, large amount; 3, medium amount; 2, small amount; 1, trace; 0, looked for, none found.
*Data Source:*  USDI—National Park Service, Western Archaeology Center, Tucson, Arizona.

TABLE 3.4
**Brick Test Results—Colorado Samples**[a]

| Soil sample | Description—appearance | Soil analysis[b] | | | | Brick test results[b] | | | | | |
| | | Gravel (%) | Sand (%) | Silt (%) | Clay (%) | Brick code | Note | Sample No. | Comp. Str. PSI | Mod. Rupt. | Drop[c] test |
|---|---|---|---|---|---|---|---|---|---|---|---|
| | | | | | | | | | | | |
| | | | | *Manassa, Colorado* | | | | | | | |
| #2 | A&J yard top soil, with roots, sticky, thin layer (6–8 in.), black organic | ? | 43.0 | 44.8  12.2 57.0 | | — | W/roots W/O roots | — — | — — | — — | — Passed |
| #3 | City of Manassa surplus soil clean, slightly sandy | ? | 65.6 | 22.2  12.2 44.4 | | E | Straw added W/O straw | E-1 — | 374 — | 24 — | Passed Passed |
| #4 | A&J standard adobe mix, estimated to be 70% "sand" + 30% "clay". Bricks crack when drying too fast from wind | ? | 69.3 | 16.0  14.7 30.7 | | F | | F-1 F-2 | 376 397 | 43 57 | Passed ? |
| #7 | A&J modified mix, estimated to be 80% "sand" + 20% "clay". Minimal cracking on drying | ? | 71.4 | 12.7  15.9 28.6 | | D | | D-1 D-2 | 302 291 | — — | Failed (defective brick) |
| | | | | | | | | | | | |
| | | | | *Salida, Colorado* | | | | | | | |
| #13 | Bank run, large stones, few fines, doubtful appearance | ? | 81.4 | 11.4  7.2 18.6 | | B | | B-1 | 333 | 70 | Passed |
| #14 | Crusher tailings, uniform size sandy, minimum clay, clean | ? | 83.9 | 10.2  5.9 16.1 | | A | 12% soil #15 88% soil #14 | A-1 A-2 | 172 178 | 49 — | Passed |
| #15 | Old "clay" pit for brick manufacturing white, chunks, small stones | ? | 72.6 | 11.5  15.9 27.4 | | — | | — | — | — | — |
| #17 | Mixture sample: Crusher tail, 80%; "Adobe Park Clay", 20%. Appears to be an ideal mix | ? | 77.6 | 14.0  8.4 22.4 | | C | | C-1 C-2 C-3 | 192 207 241 | 89 70 — | Passed |
| | | | | | | | | | | | |
| | | | | *Castle Rock, Colorado* | | | | | | | |
| #20 | Pumice appearance, grainy, few fines, from south side of Middle Knoll | ? | 86.4 | 5.2  8.4 13.6  #26  58.7 avg | | G | 80%-#20 20%-#26 | G-1 G-2 G-3 | 309 268 246 | 74 52 — | Passed |
| #21 | Clay appearance, 6 in. below surface from south side of Middle Knoll | ? | 42.6 | 36.5  20.9 57.4 | | — | | — | — | — | — |
| #24 | Dry sample, clayey looking top soil, from 75 ft. south of "pumice" area | ? | 86.4 | 5.2  8.4 13.6 | | H | | H-1 | 289 | 74 | Passed |
| #25 | Heavy "clay"—east face at road cut. Middle Knoll sticky, slow dry, massive cracking | ? | 56.4 | 18.9  24.7 43.6 | | — | Addn. of straw reduced cracking to accept. level | — | — | — | — |
| #26 | Top soil, apparent "clay"—from N. side of Middle Knoll | ? | 41.3 | 31.5  27.2 58.7 | | — | See #20 above | — | — | — | — |
| #32 | "Clay and sand"—from Compton's | ? | 82.6 | 7.7  9.7 17.4 | | I | | I-1 I-2 | 157 170 | 67 — | Passed |

[a] Preliminary draft: Solar Adobe Masonry Systems, DOE, Colorado, 1981.
[b] Natural Resources Laboratory, Inc., Golden, Colorado, 8/26/81, 8/19/81.
Particle size: USDA Std. clay, less than 0.002 mm; silt, 0.002 to 0.005 mm; sand, over 0.005 mm. —, not tested.
[c] Drop test: passed, no damage, chipped corner; failed, shattered, broke in two or more pieces.

**PARTICLE SIZE**     The State of New Mexico Building Code for adobe formerly restricted the particle size of material used to a minimum of 25% and a maximum of 45% passing a #200 screen, but has been deleted in 1982. This requirement appears unnecessary in view of tests conducted in Colorado under a DOE Grant (#DE-FG48-81R801008). The purpose of the study was to determine the feasibility of making bricks and building test structures at random locations in several climatic zones, using naturally occurring soils at each site. Soils were chosen for making sample bricks that ranged from almost total gravel (Fig. 3.1b), with few fines, to a heavy clay with a very small percentage of aggregates or sand. Subsequent laboratory tests of the sample bricks indicated good test performance from seemingly unsuitable soils (Fig. 3.3; Table 3.4), and the performance of the test structures demonstrated their weathering qualities as well. The main rationale for the test was the possible economic needs for buildings at random sites, rather than by choosing sites with "adobe" soils. At each site, random soils were chosen from within 100 ft of the proposed construction, and bricks made from these soils. The soils were first used as naturally occurring without modification, then in combination with other soils in the immediate vicinity, and finally some were tempered with straw where it appeared that the clay content was too high. In each case, the soil makeup for each type was analyzed, and sample bricks of the soils were tested. Simple test structures were constructed to provide typical exposure patterns to the elements, using various combinations of bricks in each structure. The test structures were then monitored for a period of one year, and the study is ongoing (Fig. 3.4). It may be concluded that the particle size and clay content are of minimal importance. Richard Clough, in his study[1] concludes: "Mechanical analysis of a soil is not an infallible index as to the soil's behavior in an earth wall."

FIGURE 3.3. **Test bricks, Salida, Colorado, 1981. (a) These test bricks were molded from the high gravel soil in the background. (b) A close-up of the partially dry bricks.**

FIGURE 3.4. **Test structure, Salida, Colorado, 1981. This test structure, 24 in. × 24 in. × 4 ft is being observed through one year. Standard concrete foundations and a concrete block cap were incorporated to exclude any extraneous weathering effects on the test structure. Several soil mixtures were used in various courses of the brick, none of which evidenced any measurable weathering during the first year.**

**CLAY TYPES**

The types of clay found in different geographic areas are often mixed, each having different characteristics. Some clays expand greatly with the addition of water or moisture, and some are inert. The clay type may be accurately analyzed by X-ray diffraction, but simple field tests may indicate the expansion or shrinkage when placed in a mold and dried. The most common clay types are classified as follows:

Montmorillinite: **Extremely expansive**
Mica
Vermiculite
Chlorite
Kaolin: **Inert**
Interstratified

Classification of quantities detected in tests are typically noted as:

5. Dominant
4. Large amount
3. Medium amount
2. Small amount
1. Trace amount
0. Looked for, not detected

While the type of clay present might be of importance, the practical requirements would seem to place little importance on this element. The ambient rainfall will only dampen the surface of an earth structure, and normally does not penetrate to a depth where wall movement would occur. If the wall is subjected to standing or running water, the surface can erode rapidly, and the moisture may penetrate, resulting in structural failure, regardless of the type of clay. If some other structural element is present such as cement plaster, providing a structural supporting shield, the supporting element may prevent collapse (Fig. 3.5).

**TEMPERING**     Many of the naturally occurring soils will not be ideal for the making of bricks and mortar. The proportions of sand, silt, and clay will vary in the ground. If these quantities are extreme, the soil must be tempered or balanced by the addition of another material.

FIGURE 3.5. **Flooded adobe home, Corrales, New Mexico, 1975. This stuccoed wall was inundated by a flood to a depth of approximately 3 ft for more than 24 hours. Although the wall was totally soaked with water all the way through, no structural damage occurred. Compressive strength of the adobe bricks was reduced to almost zero, but collapse was prevented by the plaster on both sides.**

If the soil has too little clay, the least common situation, a nearby source of higher clay material usually can be found. This high clay material can be stockpiled and added as tempering is required. If there is too much clay, the most common case, sand may be added, if it is available at reasonable cost. If sand is not readily available, straw, hay, or other fibrous vegetal matter may be used for tempering.

The amount to be added must be determined by the making of sample bricks. As earlier stated, the highest amount of clay that doesn't result in excessive cracking and undue shrinkage is the most desirable. Tempering should only be added to the point that cracking reaches acceptable levels (Fig. 3.6).

While it might seem difficult to determine the proper proportions of clay and sand, it really is not. The proper proportions must initially be determined by trial and error, and tested with the making of sample bricks. The person mixing the material will begin to identify clay proportions by feel and appearance. High clay material will feel greasy and will be heavy and sticky, clinging to the surface of the equipment and tools. A simple test can be made during mixing, with a brick trowel. The trowel is loaded with the mud mixture and shaken or snapped to level the mortar on the trowel. When the trowel is tilted at approximately a 45° angle, the stickiness of the clay will allow the mud to cling to the trowel. Very high clay material will stick and not come off except by scraping. As high clay material is tempered, it will begin to slide more readily, leaving behind less and less of the sticky clay material. It can be seen in the form of streaks (Fig. 3.7). This test will work more easily with sand tempering materials but will also work with straw or vegetal material.

In mixing test batches, best results can be accomplished with a wheelbarrow and a shovel. Reasonably accurate proportions between basic materials and tempering material can be measured to obtain a controlled mixture. It

FIGURE 3.6. **Test bricks, Castle Rock, Colorado, 1981. (a) Test bricks were made from extremely high clay soil, which developed large shrinkage cracks almost immediately after molding. (b) A few handfuls of straw added to the high clay soil used in (a) above reduced cracking to acceptable levels.**

FIGURE 3.7. **Trowel test for clay content.** (*a*) **A masons trowel turned at an angle will hold adobe mud with a high clay content, the clay sticking to the trowel.** (*b*) **Sand tempering of the high clay soil will allow the mud mixture to slide off the trowel easily. The comparison of stickiness indicates clay content. Bruce McHenry photos.**

must be remembered that the mix can have a broad tolerance of proportions without affecting its suitability and need not be precise. Other, larger measuring devices (front end loader scoop) will be adequate once the initial proportions have been determined. As in all construction skills, personal judgement must be a factor. This is a skill that can be easily learned with minimum experience. (Also see chapter four.)

**SUMMARY**

1. Soils that are adequate for earth walls can be found almost anywhere.
2. Identify and locate soil sources as close to the building site as possible, if the bricks are to be made on site.
3. Make sample bricks, adding tempering agent as required. Simple field tests can verify their usability after curing. (See details in chapter four.)

**REFERENCE**

1. Richard H. Clough, *A Qualitative Comparison of Rammed Earth and Sun Dried Adobe Brick*, University of New Mexico Press, Albuquerque, 1950, p. 61.

*chapter four*
# Adobe Brick Manufacturing

Adobe bricks are often compared with rammed earth as a choice for wall construction. The major requirement for adobe bricks is a climatic one. There must be certain periods of dry weather in which to mold and cure the bricks, giving rise to the widely held opinion that the use of adobe bricks is limited to arid lands. This is not necessarily so. Any area that has a climate offering periods of a week or more without rain will be adequate. Adobe brick construction also offers simple structural solutions for vaults, domes, and arches that would not be possible, or at least extremely difficult, with rammed earth.

Adobe bricks can be made from a wide variety of soils (chapter three). The manufacturing operation can be established at a number of different levels, primarily dependent on the quantity of bricks needed and the capital available for investment in manufacturing tools.

**SEQUENCE OF MANUFACTURE**

The brick-making process can be separated into a series of distinct steps or tasks. Depending on the method selected, some may be combined in order to save work or expense.

**Soil Source or Stockpile**

The soil source may be located on the building site itself, obtained from excavation of basements, cesspools, and so forth or from surplus soil from site grading. This may leave an unsightly hole. If the soil source is located away from the building site, it must be stockpiled at the point of manufacture. The physical layout of the manufacturing operation must be carefully planned to avoid additional handling of the material and finished bricks.

**Material Handling**     The material must be delivered from the stockpile to the soak pit or point of mixing. If small, on site manufacturing is to be done, the soak pit can often be the excavation itself, saving several steps.

**Mud Mixing**     The simplest method is by the use of a soak pit. The material can be mixed by hand (feet) or by mechanical means. If stabilizers are to be added, some quantitative measuring method must be established to control quality and uniformity. Water measurement can be used as a measure of control for additives. The passage element of time can also aid the mixing process, allowing the clay in the soil mixture to absorb the water (Fig. 4.1A). If the pit is flooded at the end of the work day and allowed to soak overnight, it will facilitate the mixing process the following day. The soil for bricks or mortar may be mixed rapidly by hand, without a soak pit (Fig. 4.1B).

A concrete mixer can also be used for mixing. A transit mixing concrete truck can mix and deliver material to the molding site. Concrete mixers will turn the material rather than stirring it and should be considered only for large batch mixing. A plaster mixer, which stirs the mixture instead of tumbling it, can also be used. However, for a plaster mixer to be useful, the mix must be much more liquid or the mixer will not be powerful enough to stir it. The mix from a plaster mixer can be used for brick molding, but the wetness of the mix will require additional time for drying. This will require a larger number of forms. Plaster mixer material is normally too wet to use as mortar.

Most mechanical mixers are not cost or labor effective unless large quantities of material are worked, and high production goals required. The hand process, particularly for mixing mortar, while apparently more time consuming, may be the best choice.

A. SOAKING-MIXING PIT

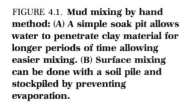

FIGURE 4.1. **Mud mixing by hand method: (A) A simple soak pit allows water to penetrate clay material for longer periods of time allowing easier mixing. (B) Surface mixing can be done with a soil pile and stockpiled by preventing evaporation.**

B. SURFACE MIXING

Water from virtually any source will be satisfactory, but it should be low in dissolved salts. Moisture from the dampness of the bricks and mortar will migrate to the surface as it dries. Upon drying, the salt crystals will recrystalize and can do physical damage to the surface of the brick. This may also occur years later, when alternate periods of high humidity may penetrate the brick. Dry periods and the addition of heating equipment in the building may cause salt recrystalization damage to the surface. Extremely brackish water should not be used for mixing bricks or mortar.

**Water for Mixing**

Delivery of the mud mixture for brick molding must be done by wheelbarrow or mechanical material-handling equipment, except in the most limited hand manufacturing processes.

**Delivery for Molding**

In molding bricks, a choice between liquid or damp mud must be made at the outset. This will be determined by the number of forms available and the expected daily production. The mixture for molding must be well mixed and uniform, or it may create dry or weak bands in the molded brick. It is more difficult to thoroughly mix a stiff mixture than a liquid one. The quality of the brick is dependent on its density, so that a wet mixture is more likely to make better bricks. If only a small number of forms are available, they must be removed more rapidly, and a mud mixture must be prepared that is stiff enough to prevent slumping when the molds are removed.

**Molding**

The ground on which the molds are placed must be level and uniform to insure consistent thickness of the bricks. A large gang form will require more careful ground preparation than a short mold (Fig. 4.2). If the ground is hard

FIGURE 4.2. **Typical adobe production yard, Alameda, New Mexico, 1971. Gang molds are filled by front-end loader. Poor surface preparation allows mud to run out at the bottom. Dirty molds and poor ground preparation produce irregular bricks.**

[61]

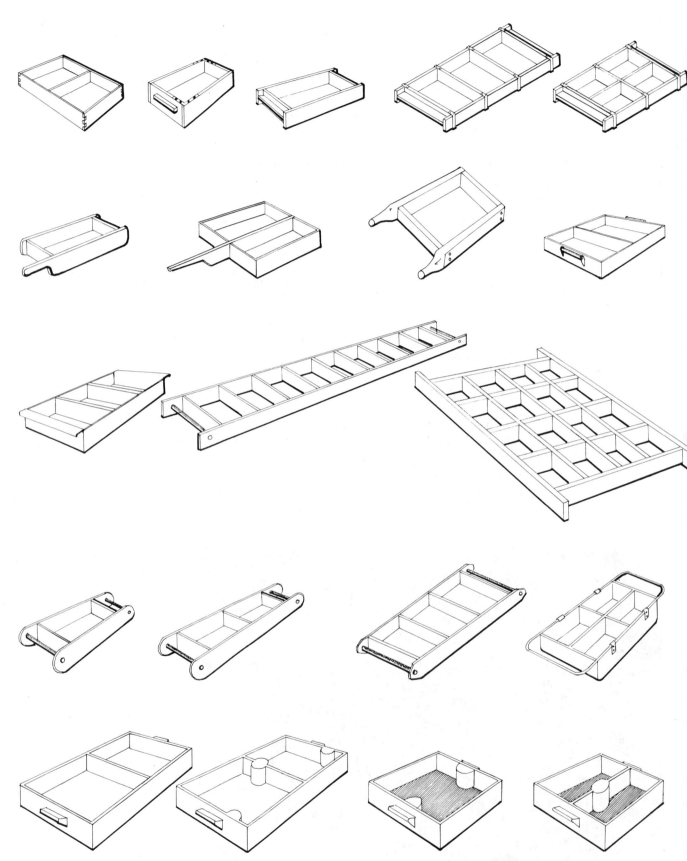

FIGURE 4.3. Typical types of adobe molds. Many sizes and configurations are in use in different parts of the world. Special shapes may be easily produced by special molds. Illustration courtesy CONSTRUIRE EN TERRE CRATerre, Grenoble, France.

or difficult to level, small irregularities may be reduced or eliminated by putting dry sand in the bottoms of the mold prior to filling, to close voids where the bottom of the mold touches the ground. It further acts as a separation compound to aid release of the bricks from the ground when turned for drying.

After the mold is filled, the top of the brick is leveled to the top of the mold by scraping or screeding.

If a stiff mixture is used, care must be taken to insure that the corners of the mold are filled, by tamping. A more liquid mixture will accomplish this without additional work.

The molds are most commonly made of wood, but can be of metal as well. They should have handles for lifting. Various types of forms are used (Fig. 4.3). If made of wood, the molds are normally soaked in waste oil to aid separation, although simple wetting will also do. The form must be cleaned regularly, or the dried mud will affect the stripping of the molds and may cause irregularities in the bricks. In some primitive societies where no equipment is available, a single brick mold is used, with a bottom on it. In this manner, the mold can be filled, carried to the molding location and turned upside down, leaving the brick on the ground for drying. Metal is sometimes used to line the molds, easing cleaning and separation.

**Initial Drying**

After molding, the bricks are flat on the ground surface and the molds have been removed. They must remain in this position until they are dry enough to handle. This initial drying time may be anywhere from 2–3 days in the hot summer weather, to several weeks in the winter. All the time that the bricks are in this position they are very vulnerable to rain storms, which may erode the surface and corners or dissolve them completely by flooding. In any event, rain will slow the drying time. Drying bricks may be temporarily protected by tarps or plastic sheeting, but these must be removed for curing to continue.

Care should be taken in the planning of the yard where the bricks are to be molded. Ground grades and drainage should be established so that rain water runoff will not collect or channel through the molded bricks.

**Turning and Cleaning**

The handleability of the bricks must be determined, because if they are not adequately cured, they will be extremely fragile and will break. When it has been determined that the bricks are dry enough to handle, they should be tipped and placed on edge, exposing the other larger side for drying. At the time they are tipped they should be cleaned, trimming any excess or splash from the soft bricks. This is easily done at this point, and will become more difficult to accomplish later. After the bricks are dry in appearance, they may be tested for dryness by inserting a pocket knife. The surface may appear dry, while the interior of the brick is still quite damp. This portion of the manufacturing process is the most taxing from a labor standpoint, as it involves "stoop" labor, and cannot be done in any other way. One large adobe manufacturing yard in the Southwest has found a way of producing bricks that is mutually profitable for both the company and the community. People who normally have a difficult time finding employment, such as the mentally retarded, are gainfully employed to "finish" the bricks.

**Stacking**

Curing will not be fully complete after turning of the bricks, and they may be further and completely cured in the stack. They are extremely fragile until completely dry. The bricks must be stacked on edge to prevent undue breakage, and must be handled carefully. It must be remembered that adobe bricks have low tensile strength and great weight. If the bricks are stacked flat and additional bricks stacked on top of them, the irregularities of the brick surface can set up tensile stresses and break them. A typical stacking pattern is illustrated in Fig. 4.4. If stacking and loading patterns are carefully determined, handling costs can be minimized.

Some adobe manufacturers have established palletizing procedures, where the bricks are stacked finally on a pallet. The palletizing requires that some of the bricks be stacked flat for stability, increasing the probability of breakage, but the pallets can then be handled with fork lifts and mechanical handling equipment. If pallets are made of hardwood and the bricks are uniform and of good quality, breakage may be held to 2–3% (Fig. 4.5).

**Size**

The size of the bricks to be produced can be determined by the need and the basic use to which they will be put. A number of common sizes and weights are shown in Table 4.1.

FIGURE 4.4. Adobe stockpile. Bricks are best stacked on edge to reduce breakage. A well-drained site is important to prevent ground-water damage. Rainfall will do minimal damage to edges of stockpile, but the top should be protected. Adobe stacked this way may be stored for years with minimal damage. Bricks must never be stacked more than two stacks thick. This allows air circulation.

FIGURE 4.5. **Palletizing. Good-quality bricks may be palletized for mechanical loading equipment with minimum breakage. Note the bricks stacked on edge.**

TABLE 4.1
**Common Sizes and Weights of Adobe Bricks**

| Type of adobe | Dimensions (in.) | Weight (lb) |
|---|---|---|
| Egyptian brick | 3 × 5 × 10 | 8 |
| Veneer brick | 4 × 4 × 16 | 26 |
| Half adobe | 4 × 4 × 8 | 23 |
| Burnt adobe (Las Palomas, Mexico) | 8 × 3½ × 16 | 30 |
| New Mexico standard adobe | 4 × 10 × 14 | 30 |
| Adobe (old style) | 4 × 5½ × 16 | 28 |
| Adobe (old style) | 4 × 12 × 18 | 50 |
| Mexico (standard Las Palomas adobe) | 3½ × 10 × 16 | 35 |
| Taos standard adobe | 4 × 8 × 12 | 26 |
| Hydra Brikcrete pressed adobe | 3⅝ × 10 × 14 | 30 |
| Porta Press pressed adobe | 3 × 10 × 14 | 35 |
| Terrón (Isleta Pueblo) | 7 × 7 × 14 | 35 |
| Dome brick (mosque) | 2 × 10 × 6 | 8 |
| CINVA-Ram pressed adobe | 3¾ × 5½ × 11½ | 20 |

From Adobe Bricks in New Mexico, Edward W. Smith, New Mexico Bureau of Mines and
   Mineral Resources, 1982

The precise size determination will be a compromise between the following factors:

**Modularity**

Ideal masonry units should be twice as long as they are wide, with allowance for mortar joints, to insure maximum bonding (overlapping) of the bricks as laid, with a minimum of cutting bricks to special sizes. The cutting of adobe bricks is much simpler than with standard masonry units however, and can be done with a trowel or hatchet. Certain optimum sizes may be more desirable for vault and dome structural forms. Special sizes can be made easily by the investment in additional forms.

[65]

**Weight**      The weight of the bricks is an important factor in the efficiency of the mason. While most masonry labor costs are based on the number of units laid per day, regardless of size, it might seem logical to make them as large as possible to gain more production. There are limits however, and when the weight of individual bricks increases, it will affect labor production. An optimum maximum weight is in the range of 30–40 lb. If a building design is of low profile requiring minimum scaffolding, the bricks can be larger and therefore heavier. As the height of the structure increases, the weight of handling each brick becomes more difficult. The low tensile strength may impair palletizing, and the possibility for the use of mechanical equipment may be limited. A great amount of material handling by hand must be anticipated. Vaulted structural forms are more practical with smaller bricks, mainly because of their weight (chapter ten).

**Wall Design**      The wall design must recognize the brick modules available, whether it be made of single or multiple bricks, Special sizes may be required for particular designs.

**Curing Time**      The smaller and thinner the brick, the more rapidly it will cure. The curing of the bricks is a physical process rather than a chemical one. The speed at which it happens is determined by the temperature, humidity, wind, and thickness. As the bricks are vulnerable in the curing process prior to stacking, any steps than can be taken to reduce the curing time are desirable.

Most adobe bricks in use in the United States have a nominal thickness of 4 in. (10 cm), and a weight of 30–35 lb. These require a minimum drying time between molding and stacking of at least 7 days, under the most ideal conditions. The process may take 4–6 weeks in the winter, with the possible additional complications of snow and freezing. In the Middle East, a common size is 10 in. × 10 in. × 2 in. ($25 \times 25 \times 5$ cm$^3$). This brick will weigh approximately 12 lbs and will cure in less than 24 hours, and will be light enough for throwing to scaffold height. It also offers great flexibility in design for vaulted structures, allowing 50% bonding dimension for corners, "T"s, and crosses.

Wind, during the early initial drying period, may affect the exposed surface of the bricks. This will be evidenced by the formation of excessive cracks on the surface, similar to the effect wind has on concrete slabs. If this begins to occur, it may be necessary to place tarps or protective sheeting over the bricks until the wind subsides. This will retard the curing time, and coverings should be removed as soon as possible.

Freezing weather during the drying period may cause damage to the bricks (Fig. 4.6). If extreme freezing periods are anticipated, brick molding should be postponed until warmer weather. Most adobe yards in New Mexico stop brick production in October and do not resume until late February or March. Brick molding in moderately cold seasons, with temperatures at or only slightly below freezing may be done, but the curing time will be slowed.

FIGURE 4.6. **Frost damaged adobes. These adobes were made in the winter and were frozen before complete drying.**

Bricks that are stacked properly need weather protection only on the top. This may be done with a strip of asphalt felt or boards held down with rocks or brick pieces to prevent wind from removing the cover. Total coverage with plastic or tarps should be avoided, as the laps or joints in the waterproof material may concentrate water flow causing serious damage. Total covering also prevents curing. Unprotected vertical surfaces will only be minimally affected by rainfall. Stacks should not be more than two bricks wide, to allow full drying. If stacks are combined, interior bricks may take on moisture from various sources and be destroyed. Bricks can be stored for years with minimum damage, if properly stacked and with rain protection only on the top of the stack.

**Storage**

A number of options are available in the level of production desired. These may range from an extremely small requirement where they may be hand made, to full-scale yard production where as many as 20,000 bricks can be made per day. Each of these options will be detailed.

**LEVELS OF PRODUCTION**

Handmade bricks can be produced with tools as simple as a shovel and a one-brick form. The efficiency can be increased by the addition of a wheelbarrow and gang forms for the bricks. A crew of two can produce 300–400 bricks per day with this method (Fig. 4.7).

**Handmade**

[**67**]

FIGURE 4.7. (*a*) Adobe brick manufacturing in Sasabe, Mexico, 1978. An arroyo floor is mined to a depth of approximately 4 ft, in which well-balanced soil is found. Note pile of high clay material at upper left for tempering when a sandy pocket is encountered. Dampened soil is covered with plastic water proofing sheets or tarps for storage to prevent evaporation and to aid water absorption. (*b*) Bricks are made with a three brick form, the mud mixture being stiff enough that the molds can be stripped at once without slumping. Note stored soil mix in background. The notch formed in some bricks makes a "sash" block, to receive frames for doors and windows.

**Semimechanized Production**

If equipment is available in the form of a plaster mixer and a quantity of gang forms (for 500 bricks or more) the production of the two people can be doubled. In order to use a plaster mixer and increase mixing speed, a very wet, almost liquid mud mix must be prepared. In this process, soil and water are put in a plaster mixer and the molds filled by pouring. Since the mix is liquid, it must dry in the mold past the point of slumping before the molds are stripped. This may require 3–4 hours. The first set of molds can be drying as additional molds are filled. By the time all molds are full, the first bricks will be dry enough to strip the molds and reset them for the next pour (Fig. 4.8).

Further mechanization can be accomplished by the use of a permanent, centrally located soak pit, a front-end loader, and a larger quantity of gang

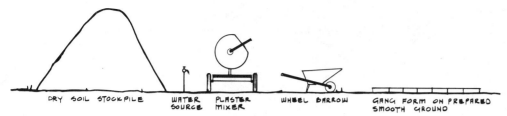

DRY SOIL STOCKPILE    WATER    PLASTER    WHEEL BARROW    GANG FORM ON PREPARED
                      SOURCE   MIXER                      SMOOTH GROUND

FIGURE 4.8. **Semimechanized production.**

molds. Soil and water can be loaded into the soak pit, and mixed by soaking overnight and by churning with the tractor wheels. The mud is placed in the molds with the front end loader, screeded smooth, and allowed to dry. If continued production at a fixed manufacturing yard is intended, the installation of a concrete floor in the soaking pit will be a valuable addition. One tractor driver and two laborers to strip, clean, and reset forms will be required. This crew of three can be expected to mold 2000 or more bricks per day (Fig. 4.9).

**Full Mechanization**

Where high volume production is to be achieved, additional items of equipment will be required. A loader–conveyor system to continuously load a pug mill (screw-type mixing conveyor) which provides a continuous supply of mixed soil and water, will provide a continuous supply of mixed material (Fig. 4.10). This mix must then be transported to a molding machine. The self-propelled type seems the most efficient, similar to concrete carriers used for pouring concrete. The mud buggies fill the hopper of a self-propelled molding machine, which fills the molds, screeds the top of the poured bricks, and returns to the position for the next mold. A machine with these capabilities is made by the Hans Sumpf Company of Fresno, California. It is most effective for large-scale production operations. With adequate backup facilities for material handling equipment and with sufficient yard space, it can produce 15,000 to 20,000 bricks per day. It incorporates features for full self-propelled mobility, permanent steel molds which can be interchanged for different size bricks and is lowered and raised hydraulically, a filling and screeding hopper which can be loaded from the side, and a self-contained water-pressure spray for cleaning molds. A Kraft paper roll on which the bricks are laid, reducing the fine grading ground preparation, is an optional feature (Fig. 4.11). Other smaller scale "adobe layers" are also available from other sources.

In our age of mechanization, inventors are constantly seeking new ways to simplify the manufacture of adobe bricks. Some of these work and some are prone to costly delays, repairs, and down time, which can seriously impair the progress of a job. The only way such a machine can be evaluated is on a basis of cost, manpower required, and the production achieved. Often the machine may not be economically viable when compared with other, simpler techniques. The following is not a complete list of adobe-molding machines, but represents only a few. If the use of such a machine is contemplated, calculate the effective cost and production carefully.

(a)

(b)

(c)

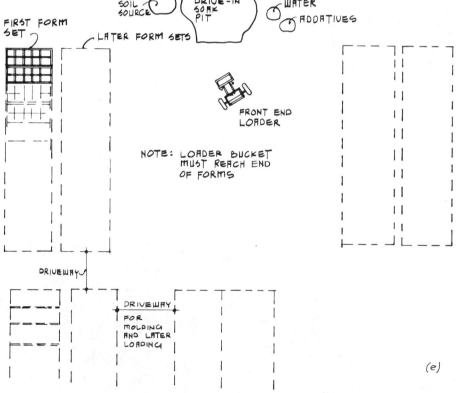

FIGURE 4.9. (*a*) **Drive-in soak pit with front-end loader.** (*b*) **Filling gang molds with loader. Note the screed rake for smoothing fill at right.** (*c*) **Filling and leveling brick pour. Note bricks tipped for drying in foreground.** (*d*) **Leveling the pour with screed rakes.** (*e*) **Yard layout for mechanized production.**

The CINVA-RAM block press has been in use for a number of years by the Peace Corps and other groups, in remote areas. It is essentially a one block mechanical press, with a lever arm. Dampened soil mixtures, not mud, are placed in the machine form, the top plate and lever are pressed down and

FIGURE 4.10. (*a*) **Mixing hopper, belt conveyor. Soil mixture is loaded into the hopper and sent to the pug mill with a belt conveyor. Bruce McHenry photo. (*b*) Pug mill. This open-type pug mill has a double screw mixer, which discharges material at the far end. A coarse screen removes larger rocks, and pipes control water flow into the dry soil. Piping to add asphalt stabilizer is also sometimes used for stabilized bricks. Bruce McHenry photo.**

(*a*)     (*b*)

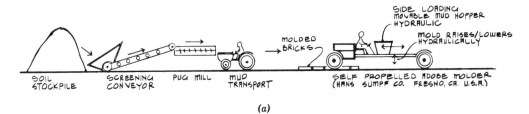

SIDE LOADING MOVABLE MUD HOPPER HYDRAULIC

MOLD RAISES/LOWERS HYDRAULICALLY

MOLDED BRICKS

SOIL STOCKPILE     SCREENING CONVEYOR     PUG MILL     MUD TRANSPORT     SELF PROPELLED ADOBE MOLDER (HANS SUMPF CO. FRESNO, CA. U.S.A.)

(*a*)

FIGURE 4.11. **Hans Sumpf adobe machine.**

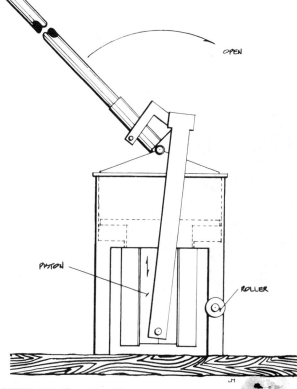

FIGURE 4.12. **Cinva Ram block press.**

released raising the molded brick for extraction. Perhaps its best use is for the manufacture of cement stabilized foundation blocks, rather than adobe bricks (Fig. 4.12).

**Hydraulic Pressing Machines**

A number of hydraulic adobe-pressing machines have been developed in recent years. They address the manufacturing problem of curing time for sun-dried bricks and humid climates, as the high initial strength may allow immediate use. These machines can also offer other economic advantages in quality control and cost. Some models also provide the capability of making bricks on the construction site, reducing handling and transportation costs.

The selection and quality control of soil types used, and the careful regulation of hydraulic pressures utilized can substantially affect the quality of the finished product. Problems have arisen with some pressed brick production, where spalling and cracking have occurred after placement in the wall. It is suspected that the problems may be related to the accretion of moisture, which in some cases results in dimensional instability, cracking, and loss of strength. Clay and aggregate types, organic material, initial moisture content, hydraulic pressure levels and the introduction of (or lack of) chemical or natural stabilizers for moisture and erosion control can be factors affecting the finished product.

The precise cause of these problems is being investigated by responsible machine manufacturers, who will supply specific test data and recommendations for manufacturing. The model shown in Fig. 4.13 is manufactured by Earth Systems International Corp., Orlando, Florida.

FIGURE 4.13. (*a, b*) **Hydraulic Block Pressing Machine. This unit produces one unit (10 × 4 × 14) every seven seconds, on the building site. Model R-1000 Photo and information courtesy of Earth Systems International Corp., Orlando, Florida**

**STABILIZATION**     The most vulnerable feature of adobe bricks is its disintegration in water. This has undoubtedly been a major point of concern since the first bricks were made. While there are many advocates for the stabilization of all bricks, the unstabilized dry bricks are not as vulnerable as they might seem. Air, humidity, moisture, and rainfall actually have little effect on fully cured bricks, as the clay limits the moisture penetration to the surface only. Standing or running water will erode the bricks rapidly and must be avoided in terms of site drainage and control of roof water run-off. If standing water or concentrated streams of water can be avoided, there is little logical reason for full stabilization. Stabilization can be defined as limiting the brick's capacity to absorb water or moisture (asphalt emulsion), or erosion proofing from water (portland cement). Bricks are normally produced in three categories:

Natural, raw, or mud adobes
Semi-stabilized adobes
Fully stabilized adobes

A wide variety of stabilizing agents for bricks, mortar, and mud floors have been used. The primary ones are portland cement, slaked lime, asphalt emulsion, vegetal juices, and a number of waterproofing chemical compounds. Although stabilization or waterproofing of the bricks may offer certain advantages, there are drawbacks as well. The principal one is that of cost. In many instances, particularly in developing nations or economically depressed areas, any stabilizing material that must be purchased for cash increases the burden greatly, or makes the project unfeasible.

Stabilized bricks in exterior walls may be justified in some cases, in that they do not require any further protection, even in problem climates. Material that has been stabilized can not be recycled, even for mortar. Another effect that has been observed is that stabilized materials may not bond well, and may not provide a homogenous mass as in the case of mud to mud. This may be due to the oxidation and evaporation of the surface after it has been exposed to air and sunlight for a period of time. No significant testing has been done in this area.

**Stabilizing Agents**

The determining factors for selection of a stabilizing agent is effectiveness and cost. The most efficient and cost effective agent to date would appear to be asphalt emulsion.

*Asphalt Emulsion*

Asphalt emulsion, once virtually a waste product, is added to the mixing water in varying percentages, depending on the basic ingredients in the soil used. Soils high in silt or clay may require more asphalt than sandier soils. The asphalt encapsulates the granular material and binds it together, preventing the infiltration and absorption of moisture. Most sandy loam soils will require 10–15% by volume for full stabilization. Partial stabilization or "semi-stabilized" bricks can be made by adding 5% or less to the water. While partial stabilization does not make the bricks waterproof, it has certain advantages, which may be cost effective for large-scale producers of adobe bricks. The partial stabilization will cause a rapid initial set of the mud after molding, and will limit rain damage at this vulnerable stage. The cost of asphalt, once a relatively minor factor, is increasing rapidly as all petroleum products increase in price.

*Portland Cement*

Portland cement may be added to the mixture to function as a stabilizer. In essence it makes a form of concrete, and if enough is added to effectively stabilize the bricks, it will increase the cost so that it approaches that of concrete. If smaller quantities are used, or it is not thoroughly mixed, long-term erosion may remove the uncemented portions, leaving voids.

*Lime*

Lime is readily available in most parts of the world either in manufactured form or as naturally occurring limestone, from which quicklime may be produced on a simple, low-tech level. Limestone is fired in a kiln and a white powder (quicklime) is produced. Quicklime is a hazardous, caustic, unstable material and must be used with caution. When water is added (slaking) to make lime putty for addition to bricks, mortar, or plaster, the mixture becomes hot, and expands to as much as five times its original volume. Most lime available commercially, in the United States at least, is "hydrated" or preslaked to reduce the hazard and expansive qualities. Research on lime indicates that the lime particles seldom achieve full slaking and expansion. Addition of water or air moisture through humidity can cause expansion, even many years after the lime plaster has originally been put in place. If large amounts of moisture are absorbed, the lime particles can expand or "blow", shattering the crystaline structure of the brick or plaster.

*Other Additives*

A number of other compounds, both organic and chemical, have been and are used for stabilization and other purposes. The addition of sodium silicates and complex plastic compounds has been attempted with some success, but in most cases the cost of the additives was too high to be economically practical. Sodium lignin sulfonate, a wood processing by-product, is sometimes added by volume producers of adobe bricks in small quantities acts as a wetting agent, and increases the speed of the water absorption by the clay. The effect of this may be similar chemically to the addition of straw.

Other organic compounds including straw, manure, blood, and plant juices have been used traditionally by vernacular builders of some cultures. The precise effect has not been examined scientifically and is unknown.

**Kiln Firing**

The hardening and waterproofing of mud bricks by heat is another form of stabilization. It can be accomplished with simple methods, and the resulting product will be resistant to erosion, but will absorb moisture. The air/sun dried bricks are stacked loosely over a fire pit area, the exterior sealed with mud plaster, and fired for several days. The resulting product, fired or "burned" adobe, will vary in quality, dependent on the temperature and length of time it was fired. In the case of a simple kiln, the quality will vary with the distance from the heat source, and the clay material used (Fig. 4.14).

The firing produces a chemical change in the brick and makes a brick that will not dissolve in water. Depending on the clay type and quantity, and the temperature acheived in firing, the brick will still have a certain water absorption capability. If the bricks are of low-fired quality, common in most primitive kilns, while not dissolvable in water, may have a high capacity for water absorption. This may not intrinsically damage the brick, but in climate areas with wide ranging daily ambient temperatures, the freeze–thaw cycles limit its use. Rain and melted snow is absorbed by the brick during warm daytime temperatures. Low nighttime temperatures will cause freezing of the moisture contained, resulting in spalling and ultimate destruction of the

FIGURE 4.14. **Simple brick kiln, Sasabe, Mexico, 1978. This wood-fired kiln is easily built and effective. The brickmaker complained that all the available firewood in the vicinity was gone and that he had to travel more than 15 miles for fuel.**

brick. Low-fired bricks, used as outdoor paving bricks, and bricks surfacing below grade walls are particularly susceptible (Fig. 4.15).

In summary, it must be concluded that stabilizers must be added to the mud mixture as it is prepared, becoming a total and homogenous part of the product. The selection of a stabilizer, if any, should be dependent on need and not just an attempt to improve the product. The additional cost of stabilizers may prohibit their use (chapter seven).

## BRICK TESTING

Laboratory testing of unburned clay masonry units is required by many code authorities. The tests required by the State of New Mexico are found in Appendix A. Additional test procedures are detailed in chapter thirteen.

The laboratory testing procedure, while not costly considering the small number of samples required for a commercial manufacturing operation, is awkward and costly for the small producer. Testing of bricks from old successful adobe structures would indicate that the tests may be unrealistic in view of the actual requirements, and perhaps unnecessary.

The only two major qualities of the brick that are important is that they be dry, and tough enough for handling and placement. Particle size, which may be limited by code, would seem to be of little importance. Compressive strength, which is commonly required to be 300 psi, seldom requires more than 10 psi in anticipated loads, plus adequate safety factors. Modulus of rupture tests represent the toughness of the brick and are usually valued at zero in structural calculations in any case. Moisture absorption for stabilized bricks is limited to less than 2% by weight and is adequate but does exceed the requirements for "frostproof" tile. Table 3.4 indicates test results from samples taken in Colorado using unlikely appearing soils. Table 4.2 is a summary of test results for all ranges of adobe bricks made in New Mexico.

FIGURE 4.15. (*a*) Home built of burned adobe, Albuquerque, New Mexico, 1982 (ca. 1958). It is suffering from frost spalling. High freeze/thaw cycles in the winter in this climate make the use of this material unwise here. (*b*) Low retaining wall, Albuquerque, New Mexico, 1982. Fired adobe suffers even more when used in a retaining wall with ground moisture. Spalling started less than one year after completion and has been repeatedly repaired. (*c*) Low retaining wall, Albuquerque, New Mexico, 1982. The higher quality frost proof bricks to the left have resisted spalling, and the ones to the right, while not true burned adobes, are not frostproof and have suffered severe damage.

TABLE 4.2
**Summary of Physical Property Tests***

| Name | Location | Type of adobe | Size of adobe (in.) | Compressive strength (psi) | Modulus of rupture (psi) | 7-day water absorption % | Moisture content % |
|---|---|---|---|---|---|---|---|
| Small-scale adobe producers | | | | | | | |
| R. Vigil | Moriarty | Traditional | 10 × 4 × 14 | 704 | 27 | — | — |
| M. Martinez | Arroyo Seco | Traditional | 8 × 4 × 12 | 486 | 49 | — | — |
| Isleta Pueblo | Isleta | Terrón | 8 × 6 × 14 | 303 | 53 | — | — |
| Frank Gutierrez | Corrales | Traditional | 10 × 4 × 14 | 312 | 45 | — | — |
| Danny Porter | Pecos | Traditional | 10 × 4 × 14 | 285 | 70 | — | — |
| Mariano Romero | Las Vegas | Traditional | 10 × 4 × 14 | 329 | 25 | — | — |
| Charles C de Baca | La Cienega | Traditional | 10 × 4 × 14 | 358 | 35 | — | — |
| D. Sandoval/E. Trujillo | Peña Blanca | Traditional | 10 × 4 × 14 | 262 | 26 | — | — |
| Edward Sandoval | Nambé | Traditional | 10 × 4 × 14 | 282 | 42 | — | — |
| Roman Valdez/James Lujan | Nambé | Traditional | 10 × 4 × 14 | 242 | no sample tested | — | — |
| Emilio Abeyta | Ranchos de Taos | Traditional | 8 × 4 × 11½ | 442 | 38 | — | — |
| Adrian Madrid | Santa Fe | Traditional | 12 × 15½ × 3½ | 391 | 33 | — | — |
| Robert Leyba | Pecos | Traditional | 10 × 3½ × 14 | 365 | 36 | — | — |
| Al Montano | La Cienega | Traditional | 10 × 3½ × 14 | 328 | 23 | — | — |
| Albert E. Baca | Namé | Traditional | 10 × 3½ × 14 | 148[a] | 32[a] | — | — |
| Albert E. Baca | Namé | Traditional | 10 × 4 × 14 | 118[a] | 18[a] | — | — |
| Joe Pacheco | Taos | Traditional | 8 × 4 × 10 | 153 | 38 | — | — |
| Felix Valdez | Cañones | Traditional | 10 × 3½ × 14 | 321 | 40 | — | — |
| Andy Trujillo | Abiquiu | Traditional | 10 × 4 × 14 | 196 | 54 | — | — |
| Aragon/Garcia Adobes | Aragon | Semistabilized | 10 × 4 × 14 | 389 | 36 | 2.0 | 1.3 |
| David Griego | Ledoux | Pressed adobe | 10 × 3½ × 14 | 1,071 | 46 | — | — |
| David Griego | Ledoux | Pressed adobe | 10 × 3⅝ × 14 | 1,036 | 58 | — | — |
| Lawrence Tenorio | Corrales | Traditional | 10 × 4 × 14 | 321 | 31 | — | — |
| Big "M" Sand & Cinder | Bernalillo | Traditional | 10 × 4 × 14 | 403 | 67 | — | — |
| D. T. Wiley | Aztec | Traditional | 10 × 4 × 14 | 500 | 89 | — | — |
| Antonio Serrano | Cañones | Traditional | 10 × 3½ × 14 | 262 | 41 | — | — |
| Humberto Camacho | Mountainair | Traditional | 10 × 4 × 18 | 556 | 56 | — | — |
| Ralph Mondragon | Ranchos de Taos | Traditional | 8 × 4 × 12 | 393 | 21 | — | — |
| Leonardo Duran | Las Palomas, Mexico | Traditional | 8 × 3½ × 16 | 484 | 13 | — | — |
| W. S. Carson | Columbus | Semistabilized | 5½ × 3¾ × 11½ | 580 | 54 | 12.7 | 2.2 |
| W. S. Carson | Columbus | Traditional | 5½ × 3¾ × 11½ | 512 | 46 | — | — |
| W. S. Carson | Columbus | Traditional | 5½ × 4 × 11½ | 769 | 69 | — | — |
| Medium-scale adobe producers | | | | | | | |
| Otero Brothers | Los Lunas | Semistabilized | 10 × 4 × 14 | 586 | 57 | 2.9 | 1.1 |
| Pete Garcia | Corrales | Traditional | 10 × 4 × 14 | 245 | 20 | — | — |
| Taos Pueblo Native Products | Taos | Traditional | 7½ × 4 × 15½ | 261 | 20 | — | — |
| Taos Pueblo Native Products | Taos | Traditional | 4 × 12 × 8 | 548 | 85 | — | — |
| Taos Pueblo Native Products | Taos | Traditional | 10 × 14 × 4 | 492 | 50 | — | — |
| Medina's Adobe Factory | Alcalde | Traditional | 10 × 3½ × 14 | 303 | 46 | — | — |
| Joe Trujillo | Ranchos de Taos | Traditional | 7½ × 4 × 10 | 615 | 68 | — | — |
| Hachita Adobe | Deming | Semistabilized | 10 × 4 × 14 | 530 | 105 | 2.2 | 1.5 |
| Rodriguez Brothers | Santa Fe | Traditional | 10 × 3½ × 14 | 714 | 36 | — | — |
| Adobeworks | Artesia | Stabilized | 10 × 4 × 14 | 320 | 74 | 1.7 | 0.4 |
| Oliver Trujillo | Nambé | Traditional | 10 × 4 × 14 | 251 | 57 | — | — |
| Robert Ortega | Dixon | Traditional | 10 × 4 × 14 | 202 | 33 | — | — |
| Alfonso Carrillo | Las Palomas, Mexico | Traditional | 8 × 3½ × 16 | 426 | 51 | — | — |
| Alfonso Carrillo | Las Palomas, Mexico | Quemado | 8 × 3½ × 16 | 644 | 180 | 15.5 | 0.5 |
| Large-scale adobe producers | | | | | | | |
| New Mexico Earth | Alameda | Traditional | 10 × 4 × 14 | 489 | 66 | — | — |
| New Mexico Earth | Alameda | Stabilized | 10 × 4 × 14 | 499 | 89 | 1.3 | 0.5 |
| Adobe Enterprises, Inc. | Albuquerque | Stabilized | 10 × 3½ × 14 | 249 | 51 | 1.7 | 0.75 |
| Eight Northern Indian Pueblos Council | San Juan Pueblo | Semistabilized | 10 × 4 × 14 | 317 | 99 | 4.3 | 0.9 |
| Eight Northern Indian Pueblos Council | San Juan Pueblo | Stabilized | 10 × 4 × 14 | 382 | 71 | 5.0 | 1.0 |
| The Adobe Patch | La Luz | Stabilized | 10 × 4 × 14 | 578 | 157 | 2.2 | 0.6 |
| Adobe Farms | Española | Stabilized | 10 × 3½ × 14 | 322 | 82 | 2.1 | 1.1 |
| Victor Montano | Santa Fe | Traditional | 10 × 3¾ × 14 | 438 | 46 | — | — |
| Western Adobe | Albuquerque | Semistabilized | 10 × 4 × 14 | 456 | 96 | 11.1 | 1.1 |
| Eloy Montano | Santa Fe | Traditional | 10 × 4 × 14 | 320 | 42 | — | — |
| Manuel Ruiz | Corrales | Traditional | 10 × 4 × 14 | 311 | 55 | — | — |
| Rio Abajo Adobe Works | Belen | Stabilized | 10 × 3½ × 14 | 486 | 101 | 1.8 | 0.76 |
| Hans Sumpf Co. | Madera, California | Stabilized | 7½ × 4 × 16 | 611 | 155 | 0.55 | 0.54 |

[a] Bricks damaged en route to testing facility.

*Note:* Tests were performed on a limited sampling of adobe bricks from each adobe yard, and the results may not be representative of total annual production. The New Mexico State Building Code recommends testing of samples selected at random from each 25,000 bricks produced. Symbol:—test not applicable. Specification requirements for Uniform Building Code and New Mexico State Building Code: *compressive strength,* average of 5 bricks—300 psi minimum, 1 out of 5 bricks—250 psi minimum; *modulus of rupture,* average of 5 bricks—50 psi minimum; *7-day water absorption,* 2.5% maximum by weight; *moisture content,* 4.0% maximum by weight.
*Data Source: Edward W. Smith, *Adobe Bricks in New Mexico,* Circular 188, New Mexico Bureau of Mines and Mineral Resources, Socorro, 1982.

FIGURE 4.16. **Knife test for dryness. (a) This brick is not fully cured (dry) and the knife penetrates. (b) This dry brick resists penetration. Bruce McHenry photos.**

**Sample Bricks**

The ultimate and final check for the suitability of any given soil is the making of several sample bricks from the soil proposed for use. These can be molded with a single or gang mold, by hand, using the soil source anticipated. Deficiencies in the material, which may require modification of the soil, may appear as the bricks are being made. A careful record should be kept of the sources and quantities of modifying materials so that the quality of satisfactory samples can be maintained in mass production after testing.

**Simple Field Tests**

The following simple field tests will give at least a preliminary indication of the brick's performance, and may be adequate to stand alone without further testing.

*Damp Test*

If a brick is dampened slightly, and a finger rubbed over the damp spot, the resistance of the brick to moisture can be somewhat determined. The degree of softening of the surface will be inversely proportional to the clay content.

*Knife Penetration Test*

The point of a common pocketknife with a small blade ($\frac{3}{8}$ in. × 2 in.) may be pressed into the side of a brick. If the brick is dry and well made, the knife will not penetrate more than $\frac{1}{8}$ in. If the brick is not dry, even though apparently dry on the surface, the knife will penetrate deeply (Fig. 4.16).

*Drop Test*

A dry brick may be dropped, on its corner, onto firm ground from a height of approximately 3 ft. The shock of striking the corner will set up stresses in the brick and indicate in-plane weaknesses or will shatter from dampness. This will approximate the modulus of rupture test, at least for toughness. In the case of a good brick, little if any damage occurs, other than a slight chipping of the corner. If the brick is not totally dry, or has weak structural planes from a lack of mixing homogenuity, it will shatter or break along the planes of weakness (Fig. 4.17).

FIGURE 4.17. **Drop test.** (*a*) **A brick dropped onto hard ground from a height of 3 ft will suffer little damage, when dropped on a corner. A flat drop could induce tensile stress from uneven ground or brick and therefore would not be valid.** (*b*) **Minimal damage, chipped corner. This brick passes the drop test.** (*Continued on page 82.*). (*c*) **This brick shattered completely when dropped, indicating that it either was not dry, or had structural planes of weakness from poor mixing or molding. Bruce McHenry photos.**

FIGURE 4.17. (*Continued*)

**SUMMARY**

1. Choose soil source carefully, with regard to quality, transportation, and handling costs.

2. Make sample bricks and determine if any tempering of the basic material will be required, testing the final product.

3. Calculate quantities of bricks required and select an appropriate manufacturing scheme. Highly mechanized manufacturing may not be cost effective.

4. If manufactured bricks are available, compare delivered costs with site made costs, space, and time requirements.

## chapter five

# Adobe Brick Wall Construction

Adobe brick walls have a number of advantages and relatively few disadvantages. Major benefits include low sound-transmission levels through walls and a general feeling of solidity and security that is difficult to describe. The thermal mass of the wall will modify and average temperature differences, a consideration in the selection of a heating, ventilating, and cooling systems. The energy investment in the basic materials is very low, adobe brick is fireproof.

The major disadvantage is the additional wall thickness which slightly reduces the ratio of usable interior space to total building space. Other materials should be considered for short partition walls and for walls that will contain plumbing stacks and other mechanical features.

The basic wall design will be influenced by a number of factors:

**BASIC DESIGN CONSIDERATIONS**

Brick size available
Wall height, thickness
Building configuration
Seismic zone
Insulation values
Architectural style and finishes
Budget

While adobe bricks can be manufactured in almost any size, standard available sizes are more economical. The design of any building that is to be made primarily of masonry must take into account the size of the brick

**Brick Size**

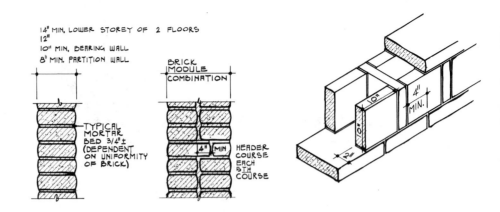

14" MIN. LOWER STOREY OF 2 FLOORS
12"
10" MIN. BEARING WALL
8" MIN. PARTITION WALL

BRICK
MODULE
COMBINATION

TYPICAL
MORTAR
BED 3/4"±
(DEPENDENT
ON UNIFORMITY
OF BRICK)

4" MIN  HEADER
COURSE
EACH
5TH
COURSE

4" MIN.

10"

2"

SINGLE BRICK
WALL

MULTIPLE BRICK
WALL

HOLLOW WALL (IRAN)

FIGURE 5.1. **Typical wall configuration.**

module (Fig. 5.1). Maximum economy is achieved with a minimum of cutting of the masonry units. With some masonry materials, not only wall thickness modules, but linear building feature dimensions and opening placement must be considered. The latter is less important in adobe masonry because the bricks may be easily cut with a trowel or hatchet and do not require a special masonry cutoff saw or costly hand chisel cuts.

**Wall Height, Thickness**

Optimum wall thickness can often be achieved with adobe masonry with single-brick wall designs, due to the larger size and stability of the brick. The wall height to thickness ratio is important for stability.

**Building Configuration**

Wall height to length ratios will be affected by the occurrence or lack of intersecting supporting walls. A lack of these may increase wall thickness or reinforcement requirements.

**Seismic Zone**

General stability and seismic requirements indicate that unreinforced wall height/wall thickness/lateral support minimums can be critical. It may be desireable to calculate seismic stability requirements for specific wall designs and expected hazards (chapter thirteen).

**Insulation Values**

Adobe walls have a relatively low insulation value, which in many cases must be augmented by additional insulation, at least on some elevations of the building that will not be subject to direct solar gain. The insolation factor from direct solar gain can be utilized if the wall is not too thick. Computer model studies indicate that the daily heat transmission curves tend to flatten out at about 12 in. (30 cm) in adobe brick walls.[1] Walls thicker than that will be proportionately higher in cost with a minimal gain in insulation value. Walls that are 12 in. or more thick will cause indoor temperatures to stabilize close to the average of the outdoor diurnal ambient air temperature variations, and will be additionally affected by direct solar gain and resulting wall surface temperatures. Additional thickness will reduce the range of daily variations of the interior temperatures, but at ever increasing cost (chapter eleven).

**Architectural Style and Finishes**

The general North American public tends to associate adobe with such typical styles common to the southwestern United States as "Pueblo" or "Spanish Territorial." This is not necessary. Adobe bricks can be used as common brick to create any style desired. The razing of old buildings in the Southwest has sometimes offered a surprise finding that Victorian residences and old commercial buildings had been built of adobe bricks and were decorated or embellished with other materials. Adobe bricks can be used as a masonry texture with or without integral masonry designs. They can be stuccoed or plastered with either conventional materials or with mud plaster and special decorative finishes.

**Budget**

The budget will of course be the final determining factor. It may be possible to realize substantial savings by the use of adobe bricks, when it has been detailed logically and simply. The low-tech nature of the material may allow the use of semiskilled labor and local resources.

**BOND BEAMS**

The use of a bond or "collar" beam should be considered, at least in the location where the roof structure is supported and attaches to the wall. Requirements in some severe seismic zones may indicate the use of additional bond/collar beams in other locations.

The bond/collar beam will serve two purposes. One is to function as a plate, spreading the concentrated roof loads over the entire wall (Fig. 5.2). The

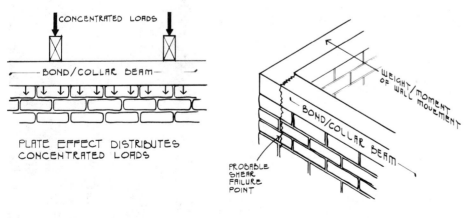

FIGURE 5.2. **Bond/collar beams.**

other is to stabilize and anchor the tops of the walls against horizontal movement. It can be made of whatever material will serve the two functions (Fig. 5.3). A third, but perhaps less significant function, is one of safety, to prevent collapse in the event of loss of a portion of the wall below. Historically, in the southwestern United States at least, it must be pointed out that bond/collar beams were seldom used. Many old structures do not have any vestige of this feature. The engineering considerations for such a beam can be analyzed (chapter thirteen).

Vernacular builders in parts of the world that are subject to severe seismic activity have sometimes dealt with collar beam reinforcing requirements by a series of smaller bond/collar beams for horizontal reinforcement, thereby reducing the stresses (Fig. 5.4).

Another consideration of the bond beam often not addressed, is its securement to the top of the wall. The weight of the bond beam, roof structure, and parapet may be sufficient without other attachment. It can be a logical point for attachment of the roof structure and will provide resistance to uplift wind forces (Fig. 5.5).

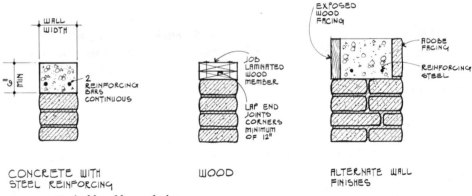

FIGURE 5.3. **Typical bond beam design.**

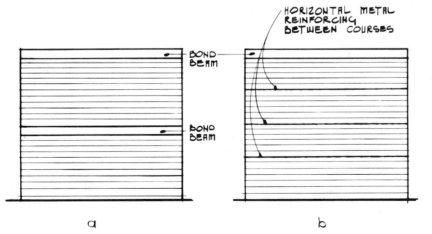

FIGURE 5.4. (*a, b*) **Multiple bond/collar beams. (*c*) Adobe chimney, Lincoln County courthouse, Lincoln, New Mexico, 1981 (ca. 1880). This tall chimney was reinforced with horizontal wood strips at 2-ft intervals, tied at the corners.**

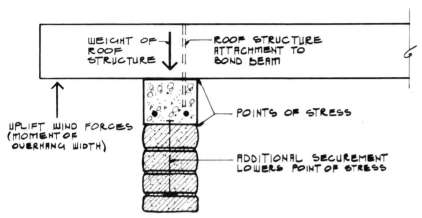

FIGURE 5.5. **Eave detail for uplift forces.**

Vertical reinforcement of adobe walls is difficult to accomplish due to the solid nature of the brick in single-brick designs. Where hollow concrete masonry units can use the void spaces in the block for location of vertical reinforcement, the solid form of the adobe brick makes this impractical except at the end joints. If the end joints are stacked and not staggered, the fabric strength of the wall is reduced. One solution proposed for high seismic-risk zones is the employment of reinforced concrete columns at corners, sides of wall openings, and at intervals in between. In this configuration, the adobe bricks become merely an infill panel, and seismic stresses work against the compressive strength of the bricks.

Multiple-brick walls can accommodate vertical reinforcing in a void between vertical walls. In this configuration, additional insulation may also be included. Care must be exercised in any construction of multiple-brick walls, making sure that the lower courses are completely dry before proceeding. The adobe bricks will absorb moisture from the mortar and will dry more slowly because less surface area is exposed. *Bricks that are or become damp all the way through have no compressive strength and may fail structurally from the weight of the wall above.* Single-brick walls dry faster and seldom present a problem. The use of lime cement mortar may help overcome this because it sets rapidly, but it still may transmit some moisture to the bricks. Too rapid curing of lime cement mortars may impair its strength. No firm rules to limit the height or number of courses laid in any given period of time can be given, as the speed of drying will be dependent on daily climate factors, mortar wetness, and so forth. The dryness of bricks in place can be verified by the simple knife test (chapter four).

If an unprotected earth wall is submerged in water, as might occur in a flood, the water will penetrate the brick and soften it at the source of the water. This can cause collapse from the wall's own weight. Concentrated streams of water from roof runoff or a direct stream from a broken pipe can also cause serious damage very rapidly. The use of waterproof coatings may trap moisture instead of allowing it to evaporate, allowing it to concentrate or penetrate even further. If bricks or rammed earth walls are fully stabilized they will be minimally affected by water. Stucco and plaster will often offer structural support for unstabilized walls.

**MORTARS**
Mortar beds for mud bricks must be full *slush* beds, where the entire surface of the brick is mortared as compared to the *ribbon* mortar beds of conventional bricks. Full slush beds will provide maximum homogenuity in the wall, giving maximum compressive strength. End or "head" joints may be filled, if the wall is to remain unplastered, or left open if plaster is to be applied. In the latter case, the voids provide a "tooth" to help support the plaster.

**Mud Mortar**
Mud mortar is made up of the same material as the bricks. Any stones more than $\frac{3}{8}$ in. (1 cm) must be removed or they may prevent the proper bedding of the bricks in the mortar. Depending on the composition of the soil used, it may be necessary to screen it before making mortar. This is a time consuming and costly process and should be avoided if possible. If a relatively small quantity of stones are found, they may be easily removed by the mason as the mortar bed is spread, by picking out larger stones with the trowel point. If this is possible, it will be more economical than the screening of the soil.

**Lime Cement Mortar**
If lime cement mortar is used, it will have the same characteristics and makeup as regular brick mortar: approximately, 8 parts sand, 1 part lime, and 2 parts cement, by volume. Cement mortar will set faster than mud mortar and allows the laying of more bricks in any one day, but this factor may represent unncessary additional cost. Cement mortar costs a great deal more and may not bond as firmly to brick surfaces as mud mortar. The only justification for its use is the speed at which it will dry.

**Lime Sand Mortar**
Lime sand mortar is similar to regular masonry mortar, but lacks the cement ingredient. Historically, this was in common use for mortars, plaster, and even concrete, when portland cement was too costly, or not available. Its primary drawback it that it is not as water-resistant as cement-fortified mortar. Lime is less costly than cement, and can be made in remote locations with limestone, a simple kiln, and adequate fuel. The resulting powder, quicklime $(CaO)$, must be slaked (soaked with water) for several days before use. It then becomes hydrated $(Ca(OH)_2)$ and is kept in putty form. The approximate proportions are: 10 parts washed sand, 2 parts lime putty, and 1 part screened earth, by volume.[2] Unwashed sand may be used after field testing to determine proper proportions.

This type of mortar is in wide use in the Middle East, where fuel supplies are limited. Raw gypsum is ground to a fine powder (#100 screen) and partially calcined (heated) to approximately 320°F, changing its chemical composition by driving off all but approximately 3% of the water. This resulting material is called *accelerator* in the gypsum wallboard manufacturing process. This mortar will set rapidly (2–3 seconds) when applying brick, and is particularly useful in the building of arches, vault structures, and the application of decorative brick or tile to vertical surfaces. Its approximate proportions are: 1 part washed sand, 1 part screened earth, and 1 part gypsum.[3] It must be mixed in small quantities, usually by hand, as the pot life is usually less than 5 minutes.

Historically the choice of lime versus gypsum based mortar seems split geographically, perhaps due to the availability of fuel. Lime kilns require very high heat, while gypsum processing, on the other hand, requires much lower temperatures for partial calcining. Traditionally, the heavily forested areas of Europe, where fuel was plentiful, used lime-based mortars, and the arid areas of the Middle East used gypsum-based mortars. In more humid regions, gypsum mortars and plasters seem to have a history of less moisture resistance over a long period of time. From a chemistry standpoint, there would seem to be no reason for choosing one in preference to the other.

**Gypsum Quick Set Mortars**

**OPENINGS**

Careful planning of the size of openings in adobe masonry is vital for maximum economy in construction costs. While openings in adobe masonry may be altered more readily than those in conventional masonry, accurate detailing of lintels, heads, jambs, and sills will avoid time consuming field modifications after the wall has been laid up. The use of rough bucks or frames may serve several purposes.

**FRAMES**

Almost all door and window openings will require a frame. The frame must be securely attached to the brick wall fabric. Metal anchors, such as nails, screws, and expansion bolts, while apparently effective initially, eventually come loose due to differences in coefficients of expansion, corrosion, or oxidation. Wood, on the other hand, seems to stay anchored securely, drying and absorbing moisture at about the same rate as the adobe bricks or mud. The most secure anchor that can be provided is either a nailing strip, laid up with the wall between courses, or a *Gringo* block (wood adobe) laid up with the wall at the point of attachment for frames (Fig. 5.6). Two or more anchors should be provided on each side of any framed opening.

One of the most time consuming tasks in masonry is the construction of plumb corners and opening sides. A rough buck, or rough frame, built precisely to receive a window or door frame, may be placed in the wall as it is laid up. This, with proper detailing, may be left in place offering more nailing points for the unit to be installed (Fig. 5.7).

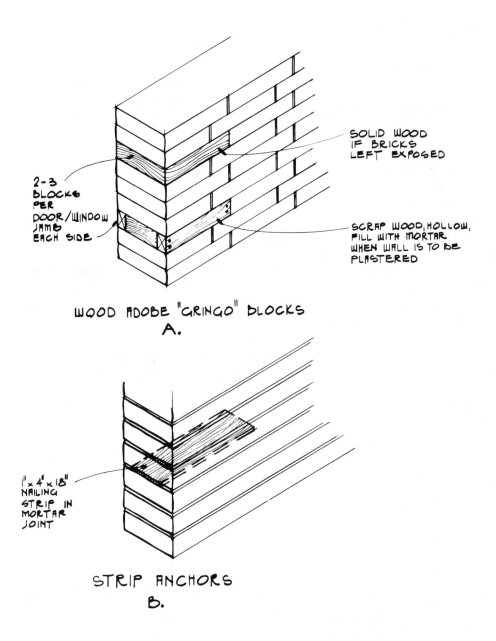

SOLID WOOD
IF BRICKS
LEFT EXPOSED

2-3
BLOCKS
PER
DOOR/WINDOW
JAMB
EACH SIDE

SCRAP WOOD, HOLLOW,
FILL WITH MORTAR
WHEN WALL IS TO BE
PLASTERED

WOOD ADOBE "GRINGO" BLOCKS
A.

1" × 4" × 18"
NAILING
STRIP IN
MORTAR
JOINT

STRIP ANCHORS
B.

FIGURE 5.6. **Wall anchors.**

**LINTELS**    Lintels over openings can be formed with a wide variety of materials and/ or arrangements. Typical detailing must indicate materials, height, and width.

**Concrete Lintels**    Lintels of concrete can be economically poured as a portion of the bond or collar beam, if ceiling heights are low enough to accomodate this. In this instance the lintel is merely a downward thickening of the bond beam, with additional horizontal reinforcement required by the opening width (Fig. 5.8).

The use of rough bucks is particularly advantageous where concrete lintels are used, as the top of the rough buck will also function as the bottom of the form for the concrete lintel. It may be left in place after pouring and will serve as a nailing anchor for the attachment of frames.

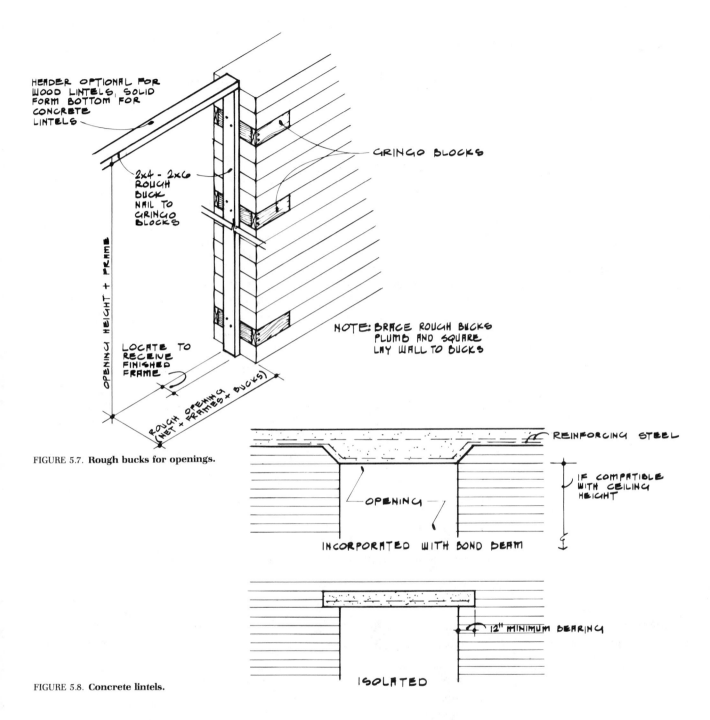

FIGURE 5.7. **Rough bucks for openings.**

FIGURE 5.8. **Concrete lintels.**

Wood lintels can either be minimal, for function, or heavier than actually required, for appearance. The lintels may be lighter in weight than commonly supposed, as the bricks above (or concrete bond beam) will offer a flat, jack-arch effect, reducing the actual loads on the lintel proper. Depending on wall height and design, the wood lintel may become a part of, or intrude into, the bond beam above. The bearing ends of the lintel, if not attached to the bond beam, must bear a minimum of 8–12 in., so that the load above may be transferred to an adequate area of the masonry wall (Fig. 5.9).

**Wood Lintels**

[91]

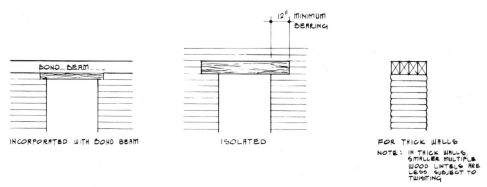

FIGURE 5.9. **Wood lintels.**

**ARCHES**    The use of arches to span opening heads can be effective, but may lead to costly problems. As most standard door and window frames are flat on top, it follows that the opening to receive them should be flat as well. Curved door and window frames and heads can be provided, but the special provision of such items will increase the cost. In arid geographic areas where wood products are scarce, expensive, or unavailable, the use of arches may be a viable solution. The curved portion at the top, which carries the structural load, can be infilled with additional masonry after the window or door frame is in place. The arch may also be useful as a decorative feature and for architectural effect (Figs. 5.10 and 5.11).

Typical full-wall elevations and detailed sections are illustrated in Figs. 5.12 and 5.13.

The rationale for traditional Islamic pointed arch forms is not clear. It may have been generated by the need to build arches without centering (support). Arches may be built with small bricks and mud mortar without support, with bricks laid to an angle as high as 70° using friction and the adhesive quality of the mud mortar to hold the bricks in place.

**QUANTITY CALCULATIONS FOR MATERIALS**    Quantities required for earth and/or bricks are normally calculated on an area basis. This may also be done volumetrically. A typical case is as follows

Brick size:   10 in. × 4 in. × 14 in. (25 × 10 × 35 cm³)
Wall thickness:   10 in. (25 cm)
Mortar joints:   Average $\frac{3}{4}$ in. (2 cm)
Wall area:   10 ft × 10 ft = 100 ft² (9.3 m²)

Area Basis:

Brick face including mortar joint: 0.435 ft² (0.04 m²)
Bricks required: 100 ft² at 0.435 ft² = 230 each
Mortar: 230 bricks × 110.6 in.³ = 14.7 ft³ = 0.55 yd³
Water for mortar: 20–30 gal/yd³ × 0.55 yd³ = 11–16 gal.

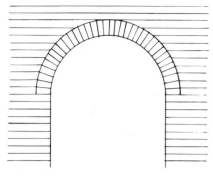

HEMISPHERICAL ARCHED OPENING

RISE 1/8" PER FOOT OF SPAN FOR FLAT OPTICAL ILLUSION

CAMBER ARCH

FIGURE 5.10. **Arches.**

FIGURE 5.11. **Plywood arch form, Dar Al Islam Mosque, Abiquiu, New Mexico, 1981. Standard size forms were built for project use, and could be reused. While the arch may be built without support, the form helps insure uniformity of pattern, and may be of light-weight material.**

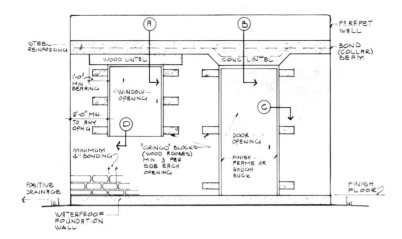

FIGURE 5.12. **Typical wall elevation.**

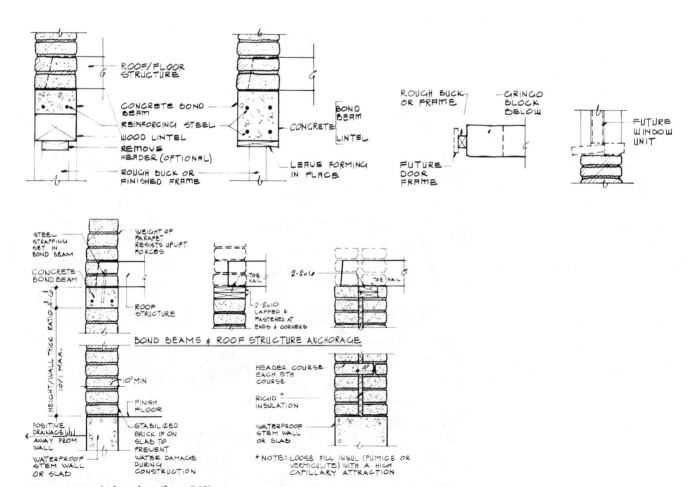

FIGURE 5.13. **Typical sections (from 5.12).**
**Typical full-wall sections.**

Efficient production in the erection of adobe masonry is much the same as in other masonry-labor crew organizations. Several distinct tasks are required:

Mortar mixing
Mortar delivery to the wall
Brick delivery to the wall
Brick setting
Striking and/or cleaning of excess mortar from brick joints

Each mason should have a mason tender, or assistant, who keeps supplies of bricks and mortar within arm's length of the mason laying brick. Any interruption of the mason's rhythm will slow production. Adobe bricks are heavy, and any arrangement to reduce handling costs will be beneficial. For example, when bricks are delivered to the site, it is advantageous to unload them adjacent to the wall where they will be laid. Sometimes the physical topography or constriction of the site will not permit this. If the bricks are unloaded in any other location, they must be moved by hand (brick barrow) to a location where they are in reach of the mason. The mud mixing for mortar can best be done at several points so that the transportation of mud can be held to minimum distances. It may be best to locate one mud pit at each corner of the building. The multiple locations will also offer the advantage of allowing additional soaking time in a pit that is not in use (Fig. 5.14).

The mason tender can deliver mud to the wall, usually in a wheelbarrow, redistribute bricks as necessary to arm's length of the mason, and further make the initial spread of mortar on the top of the wall being laid, with a

**LABOR PRODUCTION QUANTITIES**

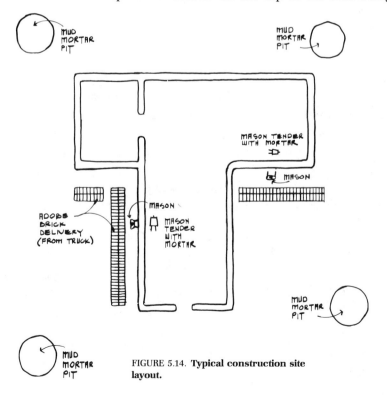

FIGURE 5.14. **Typical construction site layout.**

shovel. This can best be done from the opposite side from which the mason is working. In slack periods, the mason tender can assist the mason in filling and striking mud from the joints. A "story" pole at each corner of the building, showing the height of each course, will speed production.

One person should be responsible for the mud mortar mixing to insure proper quality and consistency. One mortar mixer can provide mortar for at least two mason/tender teams. If bricks cannot be unloaded close to the walls, additional material-handling labor will be required. The production rhythm must be established, and the sum of the labor of the team will result in more production than two people trying to do each of the several tasks independently, breaking the rhythm.

A typical team:

Mason
Mason tender
Mud mixer, helper

Production of such a team should be:

400–800 bricks/day—shoulder high
200–400 bricks/day—on scaffold

As the height of the wall increases, so do the handling costs of the brick, resulting in lower production rates. Mechanical hoisting equipment may sometimes be used to advantage, but the weight of the bricks placed in quantity on a scaffold or roof deck could cause problems. The cost of utilizing mechanical equipment may outweigh the cost of doing it by hand.

**SUMMARY**
1. Design wall sections for materials that are readily available and cost effective.
2. Plan material delivery and storage arrangements carefully to minimize brick and mortar handling costs.
3. If questions on seismic stability arise, make calculations to determine specific building requirements.
4. Analyze insulation-thermal mass effect with local climate and coordinate the results with the selection of mechanical heating, cooling, and ventilation systems.

**REFERENCES**
1. Francis Wessling, Transient Thermal Response of Adobe *Adobe News*, #6, Albuquerque, New Mexico, 1975.
2. P. G. McHenry, Jr., Report to National Park Service USDI July 8, 1978, Albuquerque, New Mexico.
3. P. G. McHenry, Jr., *An Examination of Mud Brick Architectural Forms in Iran with Experimental Applications in the Southwestern United States*, Master's Thesis, University of New Mexico, Albuquerque, New Mexico, 1974.

*chapter six*
# Rammed Earth Wall Construction

Rammed earth walls, or Pise', as it is termed in many French-speaking countries, is a method of simple wall building that has a long successful tradition in many parts of the world. Although its beginnings are not clear, it would seem logical to conclude that this form evolved from "puddled" mud wall construction, a prehistoric type of mud wall that developed independently in many parts of the world, and still in use today (Fig. 6.1). Rammed earth walls, placed with forms, have many similarities to adobe brick construction, but the concept is totally different.

The major differences between rammed earth wall building and adobe bricks may have originated for climatic reasons. Adobe bricks require rain-free periods of time in which to make and cure the bricks, thus placing some limitation on the geographic and climatic areas where they may be used. Rammed earth walls, on the other hand, may be constructed in more damp, humid climates where brick manufacture would be difficult or impossible. Other factors of tradition and cultural acceptance undoubtedly play a role. Rammed earth has been widely used and accepted in Australia and North Africa, arid climates in which brick would also be feasible. It is also widely used in France, and in similar more humid climates. It was also widely used on the Eastern Seaboard of the United States during the 19th Century and when manufactured materials were not available. An early manual for the construction of rammed earth walls was written in 1839 by E. Gilman called *The Economical Builder*. It extolled the virtues of this building system, declaring it to be sound and economical.

Rammed earth walls are built of soil with the proportions of aggregate, sand, silt, and clay in similar proportions to the soils used for making adobe bricks. The rammed earth method utilizes forms, usually of wood, that are

FIGURE 6.1. **Puddled mud wall, Upper Volta, Africa, 1980. Erosion shows coursing and suitability for curved-wall forms. Erosion patterns are similar to Casa Grande walls in Arizona, and in Iran. Photo courtesy Centre de Documentation Photographique sur l'Architecture. Photographie de Christin Bastin et Jacques Evrard, 127 rue de l'Abre Benit, 1050 Brussels, Belgium.**

placed and secured, and damp earth is loaded into them and tamped to total compaction. When the forms are removed, the wall is complete, except for curing, and requires no further treatment other than plaster finishes or cosmetic treatments as desired.

The major differences in rammed earth building techniques occur in the method of forming. This may range from very simple small, wooden slip forms, secured with rope or wire, to patented manufactured forming systems used in concrete. Some builders have developed ingenious and effective systems using simple forming techniques that are made from locally available materials. Any system that will provide a sturdy form will do.

**SOILS**

The soils used in rammed earth are identical to those used in adobe bricks. A soil with small gravel aggregate, sand, silt, and clay will be most suitable. The durability and waterproof qualities of the wall are dependent on the clay content, which ideally will approximate 15–18%.[1] A higher clay content is allowable and desirable in soils used for rammed earth, while adobe bricks with high clay content have a tendency to crack on drying. The moisture content is much lower initially in rammed earth and therefore less subject to shrinkage on drying (chapter three).

**Mixing—Wetting—Tempering**

Soil, as it comes from a naturally occuring ground source, frequently has adequate moisture for its use directly in rammed earth walls. It must be damp but not wet. Soil with a high moisture content will resist compaction by its fluidity and jelly-like consistency. Soil that is too dry will not result in the cohesive bonding of the particles caused by the integration of the clay and moisture. Dry layers of unconsolidated material will also cause weak structural planes within the wall structure.

If the soil source is too dry, it may be wetted prior to its use by employing sprinkler hoses and fine water sprays, so that limited quantities of water may be introduced to the source or stockpile without total soaking. The additional moisture added must be absorbed by the soil stockpile, which will be aided by time and additional mixing, either by hand or the use of mechanical equipment to stir and tumble the material, distributing the moisture more evenly. The hand-mixing method is practical but laborious, and mechanical mixing equipment is better if it is available.

Practitioners of rammed earth construction suggest that it is easier to dry soil out than to add limited amounts of moisture to it. As the soil is removed from its source, either by hand or excavation machines like a front-end loader, it will tend to dry as it is stockpiled for use.

The precise proportions of aggregate, clay and sand are not critical and a simple field test may be made to determine the readiness of a soil for use. First, it should appear damp, but not wet. A handful of the soil may be squeezed into a firm ball readily by hand. In this test, a soil with too high a moisture content will feel sticky and will not form a firm solid ball when squeezed. On the other hand, if too little moisture is present, the soil will not compact and hang together at all. The successful compacted soil ball will be firm and solid, but neither hard nor sticky (Fig. 6.2). The hand compacted soil ball may be dropped onto a firm surface from a distance of approximately 3 ft (1 m). If the soil ball shatters the moisture content is adequate (Fig. 6.3). If it does not, too much moisture is present.

FIGURE 6.2. **Soil ball test. A ball of damp (not wet) soil, squeezed in the hand should compact firmly, but not be wet or sticky. Bruce McHenry photo.**

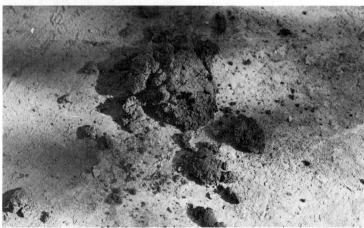

FIGURE 6.3. **Soil ball test. When the soil ball is dropped on a firm surface it should shatter, indicating that the proper amount of moisture is present. Bruce McHenry photo.**

Stabilizing agents such as portland cement may be added to the soil source to provide ultimate moisture proofing or additional strength qualities. If a basic source soil is being used, the additive may be spread out on ground surfaces where this material will be obtained. It is then turned and mixed in with a plow, rake, or mechanical device such as a rotary tiller. The mixing must be thorough, or strength and color differences may appear in the finished wall.

The most common stabilizing agents for rammed earth are portland cement and lime. If lime is used, hydrated lime is best for this purpose as compared to quicklime which will expand greatly (5–6 times) on becoming moist. Quantities of stabilizer will vary according to the basic soil makeup and may range from 5–15%. The higher, and more effective percentages may raise the cost of a wall material to that of low-quality concrete and may not be economically feasible. If stabilizers are to be added to stockpiled material, it will be necessary to spread the basic material on the ground to a measured controlled depth, add stabilizer in proportionate amounts, mix with machinery, and restockpile the stabilized mixture. It is also possible to mix the material and stabilizer in a concrete mixer to assure more uniform mixing and proportions, but the additional handling may be costly. It must also be recognized that the stabilized material will have a limited setting life, and must be placed and compacted in the wall before it sets. If more material is mixed than can be placed in a wall in a given time, the material must then be discarded.

Unless special conditions make waterproofing necessary, it would seem that stabilization is a costly procedure, with little benefit gained.

**FOUNDATIONS**   Foundations for rammed earth walls will have the same physical requirements for size and strength as their adobe counterparts. Reduced to the bare essentials, foundation walls should be at least as wide as the wall, waterproof below grade, and should be strong enough in compressive strength to support the weight of the wall and other expected loads (chapter nine).

**FORMS**   The forms used for building rammed earth walls may be simple or complex. Forms used in developing nations are often of crude, simple materials, and are generally small in size due to the limited availability of forming materials. With this type of slip form, small sections of wall are built with each setting of the forms. The small size, lighter weight, and smaller quantities of earth material are more ideal for hand labor where little mechanical equipment is available. Where available, larger, patented-type concrete forming systems are used (Fig. 6.4). There are many forms for special use, often devised by the builder, for the particular requirements of rammed earth. These special forms have features that increase their efficiency. Whatever type of

FIGURE 6.4. **Patented concrete form. Many types of concrete forms are available for use with rammed earth.**

forming system is used, special attention must be given to the securement at the bottom and top, intermediate points in the form, and at the corners.

A special type of slip form for rammed earth is recommended by Middleton (Fig. 6.5a),[1] but many other types will work (Figs. 6.5b,c). Whatever form system is used, special configurations will be required at the corners (Figs. 6.6 and 6.7), and provision must be made to accomodate window and door openings. Anchorage devices for window and door frames are best installed as the wall is rammed. The ends of the forms in a wall section being rammed need to be closed in order to obtain compaction. If a specially shaped end piece is used, it will help insure maximum stability of the connection between end joints of each rammed section by the keying of vertical end joints between pours. A special form developed by a California builder offers solid, economical forms at minimal cost, using simple materials available at most building supply houses. This type is best for jobs using maximum mechanization. Required materials are standard sheets of 1 in. (2.5 cm) plywood with a rabbeted edge for interlocking form joints, a series of "walers" made of 2 × 10's and a number of standard furniture clamps with the end retainer removed. The sheets of plywood may be cut to whatever size is required for width and height, so that the modularity of standard forms may be avoided. The sheets and walers may be reused repeatedly. It further dismantles completely, allowing reuse, full use of scrap materials, and a minimum quantity of form material (Fig. 6.8).

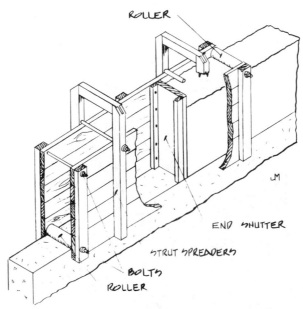

ROLLER

END SHUTTER

STRUT SPREDDERS

BOLTS

ROLLER

JM

(a) (THIS ILLUSTRATION SHOWS DOOR OPENING.)

FIGURE 6.5. (*a*) Small rolling slip form. This type of form is versatile and may be set in place and removed rapidly. The tall struts extending above the form eliminates the need for through bolting at the bottom of the form. From *Build Your House of Earth*, Middleton. (*b*) Job built forms. Concrete-type forms may also be built of conventional materials. Photo courtesy Lydia and David Miller, Rammed Earth Institute International, Greeley, Colorado. (*c*) Form stripped. After stripping, through-bolt holes and course joints for each lift can be seen. These may be rubbed out with a sponge float, or patched and coated later with plaster. Photo courtesy Lydia and David Miller, Rammed Earth Institute International, Greeley, Colorado.

(b)

FIGURE 6.6. Corner and window form. Photo courtesy Lydia and David Miller, Rammed Earth Institute International, Greeley, Colorado.

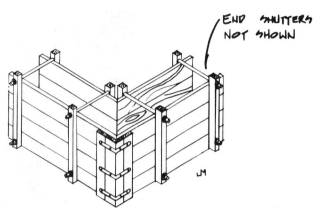

END SHUTTERS NOT SHOWN

FIGURE 6.7. Alternate corner form. From *Build Your House of Earth*, Middleton.

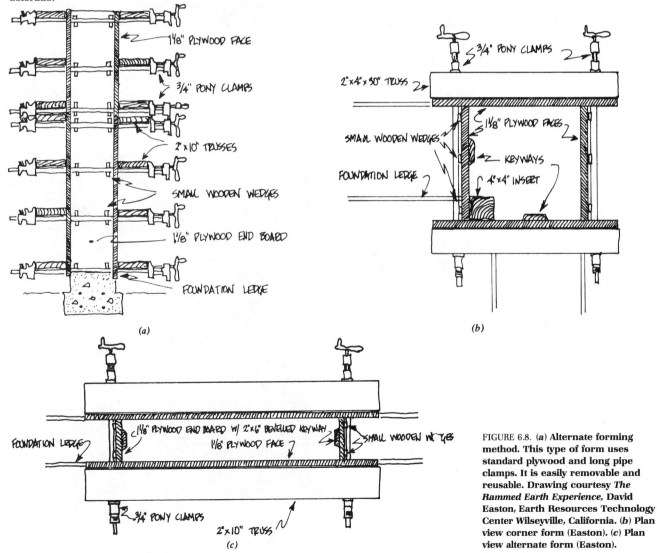

1⅛" PLYWOOD FACE

¾" PONY CLAMPS

2"x10" TRUSSES

SMALL WOODEN WEDGES

1⅛" PLYWOOD END BOARD

FOUNDATION LEDGE

(a)

¾" PONY CLAMPS

2"x4"x30" TRUSS

1⅛" PLYWOOD FACES

SMALL WOODEN WEDGES

KEYWAYS

FOUNDATION LEDGE

4"x4" INSERT

(b)

FOUNDATION LEDGE

1⅛" PLYWOOD END BOARD W/ 2"x6" BEVELLED KEYWAY

1⅛" PLYWOOD FACE

SMALL WOODEN WEDGES

¾" PONY CLAMPS

2"x10" TRUSS

(c)

FIGURE 6.8. (*a*) Alternate forming method. This type of form uses standard plywood and long pipe clamps. It is easily removable and reusable. Drawing courtesy *The Rammed Earth Experience*, David Easton, Earth Resources Technology Center Wilseyville, California. (*b*) Plan view corner form (Easton). (*c*) Plan view alternate form (Easton).

[103]

**FILLING AND COMPACTION**   When the forms are securely in place, the cavity may be filled either by hand, with a shovel or bucket, or by means of mechanical equipment. Material handling is the major task and if it is to be done by hand, adequate labor budgets or time requirements must be recognized. It will require approximately one man-hour of labor to place one cubic yd of material by shovel.[2]

The wall fill should be placed in 6–8 in. lifts, meaning that the earth fill should be placed only to a depth of 6–8 in. before compacting. After each lift has been compacted, another may be placed for compaction. The dampness of the material and the uniformity of compaction is important, or the result may be dry, crumbly bands of loose material in the wall, creating planes of structural weakness after the forms have been removed.

The tamping may be done by hand or mechanically. In the hand method, Middleton suggests that the optimum weight of a hand tamper is 18 lbs (Fig. 6.9). If the tamping device is heavier, it will require more physical effort without achieving better results. Full compaction may be determined by a change of sound or "ringing" when tamping. Pneumatic tampers require less physical labor, but will require the use of a heavy-duty air compressor and automatic tamper with a long handle (Fig. 6.10).

When the wall is compacted and the forms removed, it should be stable enough for further construction, and will have a compressive strength of approximately 30–90 psi. This will be sufficient for most anticipated loads, allowing construction to continue, but the surface and corners will be fragile until curing has occurred. Full drying or curing of the wall may require

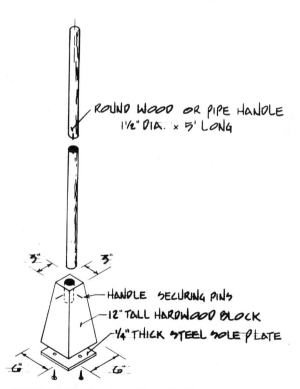

FIGURE 6.9. **Hand rammer.** From *Build Your House of Earth*, Middleton.

FIGURE 6.10. **Pneumatic tamping. Thicker walls give more room for tamping and will be more sturdy until fully dry.**

[104]

several months or even years, dependent on weather and humidity. Ultimate compressive strength should be approximately 450–800 psi. Portland cement added as a stabilizing agent will require 28 days to reach design strength and will raise the compressive strength. Dependent on wall thickness, height, and building design, this additional compressive strength may not be necessary.

**WALL DESIGN**

The principal criteria for wall design will be governed by the same guidelines that would be used for masonry or formed-concrete wall systems, recognizing the lower strength factors of earth walls. Wall height/thickness ratios for stability, a minimum of 10/1 for bearing walls, seem to be an international vernacular standard. The length of the walls, unsupported by intersecting walls, and additional seismic hazards may also affect the design. Insulation and thermal mass values are also to be considered. Preliminary studies of thermal mass properties would indicate a minimum wall thickness of 10–12 in. (25–30 cm), and a maximum of 24 in. (60 cm), although structural requirements and architectural design considerations for special situations may affect the decision. Unless it serves some other specific purpose, additional wall thickness only increases the cost of materials and labor. An evaluation of thermal properties will be found in Chapter 11, and structural considerations in Chapter 13.

**BOND AND COLLAR BEAMS**

The low tensile strength of earth walls may indicate the desirability of providing a bond or collar beam at certain locations as a means of providing horizontal reinforcement in the wall. Relatively low static compressive loads are easily handled by the strength of most earth walls, but the possibility of movement either by settling or by seismic activity may exceed the tensile strength. The bond or collar beam adds a measure of reinforcement, helping contain those stresses to smaller areas. Several materials may be considered for this task. Depending on ceiling heights, the bond beam may also be incorporated as all or a part of lintel requirements for openings.

**Concrete**

The strongest and therefore perhaps the most desirable configuration might be considered to be a steel reinforced concrete beam, poured in place, at the bearing point for roof or upper-floor structures (Fig. 6.11). The eco-

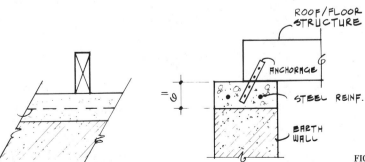

FIGURE 6.11. **Concrete bond beams.**

nomic possibilities of a given geographical area may preclude the use of a concrete bond beam, and a simpler form must be used. It must be pointed out that virtually none of the historic earth structures, many of great age, had any semblance of a bond or collar beam. Most had thicker walls than currently are constructed. Perhaps the geographic location of the surviving buildings is favorable to their survival, or perhaps the faulty ones that might have needed a bond beam have long since disappeared.

**Wood**      Wood members will function as a bond/collar beam if provision is made for the horizontal connection of its smaller elements. It may be composed of large or small segments, providing they are joined securely at the ends and corners (Fig. 6.12).

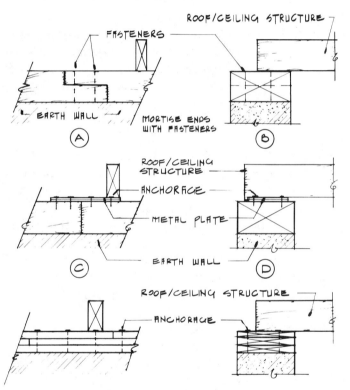

FIGURE 6.12. **Wood bond beams.**

**Steel**      Steel or wire reinforcing may also be a viable alternative for horizontal reinforcement, although it will provide less plate effect for distributing concentrated loads that the concrete or wood examples above. This reinforcing may be a patented prefabricated form of masonry reinforcement such as "DUROWALL" (ladder mesh) or even a simpler material such as barbed wire, the barbs providing additional anchorage in the wall. Deformed reinforcing steel may also be used. Smooth wire would be the least desirable (Fig. 6.13).

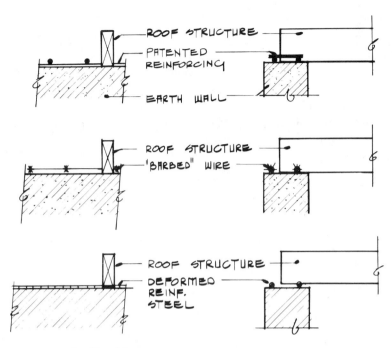

FIGURE 6.13. **Steel bond beams.**

The placement of additional reinforcement, either vertical or horizontal, is easily accomplished with a rammed earth wall. Any of the bond/collar beam types (Figs. 6.11 to 6.13) may be used, placing them as the wall is built. Vertical reinforcement may also be easily placed, compacting the wall around the reinforcing elements (Fig. 6.14). Building codes in some areas require a steel reinforced concrete column and beam structural system, using the rammed earth as infill panels. The rammed earth panels are placed first, leaving space for the columns, with the columns and beam being poured at the same time (Fig. 6.15). The additional costs in this type of wall design may overcome its advantages.

**ADDITIONAL REINFORCEMENT**

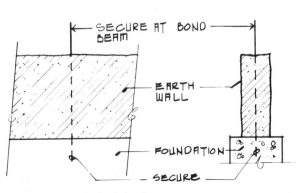

FIGURE 6.14. **Vertical reinforcing.**

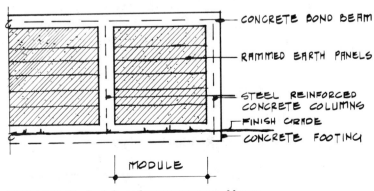

FIGURE 6.15. **Steel reinforced concrete post and beam.**

**OPENINGS**   All openings in earth walls must be provided with a lintel structure strong enough to span the opening width, and a provision for anchoring door and window jambs to the wall. Doors present more of a problem than window frames because of the vibration. While a solid, cured earth wall seems to accept metal fasteners such as nails and expansion bolt fasteners securely at inception, vibration, time, different expansion coefficients, and the oxidation effects of metal fasteners will ultimately cause a loosening of the fasteners in the wall. Solid wood anchors, placed in the wall as it is built, are less likely to cause future problems.

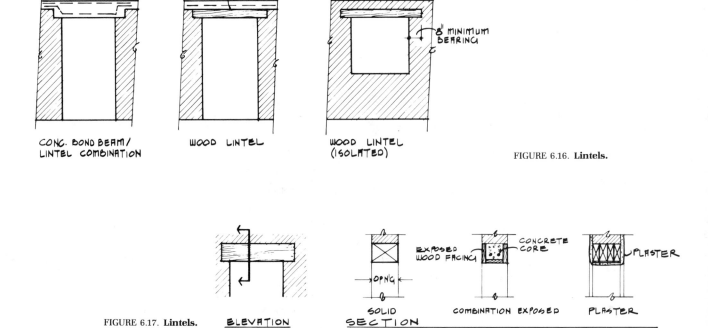

FIGURE 6.16. **Lintels.**

FIGURE 6.17. **Lintels.**

**LINTELS**   Structural and/or decorative lintels may be incorporated either as a downward extension of the bond beam, or as an isolated element, depending on ceiling height and the materials selected (Fig. 6.16). Lintel bearing, if not a part of the bond beam, should be a minimum of 8 in. (20 cm) on each side, due to the relatively low compressive strength of the earth wall. The desired finished appearance of the lintel may help determine the choice of material and system to be used (Fig. 6.17).

**FRAME ANCHORS**   When ramming the wall, a form must be secured at the jamb of the openings to contain the wall material as it is being rammed. This may consist of a rough frame, if leaving it in place will not cause finishing problems later, or might be the finished frame itself. A problem with the latter course is the possibility of physical damage to the finished material during construction. In any event, an anchoring device must be provided in the wall fabric. One simple answer is the use of a wood "T" anchor, placed as the wall is rammed (Fig. 6.18). Wood blocks may be used, or a recessed rough frame could be laid up as a part of the opening form (Fig. 6.19).

## SILLS

Sills for openings must deal with the moisture-vulnerable nature of the rammed earth wall, unless the wall material has been stabilized with a water-proofing material. In any event, the sill detailing is best installed after installation of the window or door. Positive drainage, built from water resistant materials at the sill, is recommended to carry off rain water on the exterior, so that any direct flow is carried to a drip edge and can drip free of the wall. Interior sills should also be protected from accidental rain damage, condensation collection, and physical abuse. The earth material may be easily shaped or filled to accommodate whatever sill treatment is selected.

## TYPICAL WALL SECTION

For a typical wall section refer to Fig. 6-20.

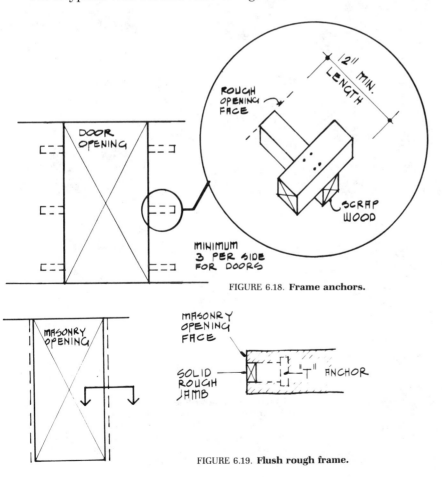

FIGURE 6.18. **Frame anchors.**

FIGURE 6.19. **Flush rough frame.**

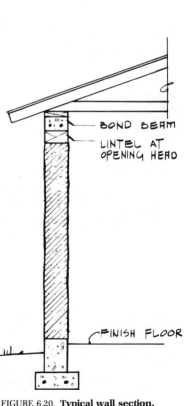

FIGURE 6.20. **Typical wall section.**

**PUDDLED MUD WALLS**         Another form of rammed earth wall construction without the use of forms is one currently used in Iran, where it is called *chine* construction. In this method, damp mud is placed and shaped by hand. The wall is built of successive layers, 18–24 in. (46–60 cm) thick and 18–24 in. (46–60 cm) high. The lower course to dry before application of the next course. This is similar to the technique used in making "coil" pottery (Fig. 6.21). Although not tests were made, it would seem that this form might not offer the higher density (i.e. compressive strength) of either adobe or of rammed earth construction. In Iran, this type of wall is most often used for garden walls rather than structural building walls. Perhaps this indicates their lack of confidence in the structural qualities of this type of wall design.

Examples of identical appearance can be found in the Western Hemisphere at Casa Grande, Arizona and Casas Grandes, Chihuahua, Mexico, dating back almost a thousand years (Figs. 6.23 and 6.24).

FIGURE 6.21. **Puddled mud wall construction, Iran, 1972. (a), (b) Mud is mixed at the side of the wall and placed by hand. After one ring is completed and adequately dry, another course is placed on top. (c) Background shows older, completely dry wall, similar in appearance to Upper Volta, Africa (Fig. 6.1) and Casa Grande, Arizona (Fig. 6.22).**

FIGURE 6.22. **Casa Grande, Arizona, 1975 (ca. 1000 A.D.). (Multistory puddled mud walls still standing after almost 1000 years.**

FIGURE 6.23. **Casas Grandes, Chihuahua, Mexico, 1979 (ca. 1000 A.D.). (a) A large community was built of puddled mud walls, using structural wood members for roof framing. (Continued on page 112.)**

FIGURE 6.24. (*Continued*) Casa Grandes, Chihuahua, Mexico. (*b*) Careful attention was paid to drainage to keep walls dry.

**SUMMARY**
1. Field test soils planned for use.
2. Determine handling/mixing procedures, quantities and labor costs, and equipment required.
3. Determine form type to be used.

**REFERENCES**
1. G. F. Middleton, *Build Your Own House of Earth* Compendium Pty Ltd. Mentone, Victoria, Australia, 1975.
2. Frank R. Walker, Ed., *The Building Estimators Reference Book*, 12th ed., Frank R. Walker, Publishers, Chicago, 1954.

## chapter seven

# Window and Door Detailing

The detailing of windows and doors in earth walls requires special consideration when compared to conventional frame and masonry construction. Most earth walls are thicker, earth wall fabric may be less uniform than conventional masonry, and the wall material is more fragile. The major enemy of earth walls is water, and careful attention to flashing and water control details is mandatory.

**DOOR JAMBS**

The door frame width and location with respect to door swing direction is the first determination. The selection of the door frame width may range from a minimum of $4\frac{1}{2}$ in. (11 cm), the standard width in the United States for frame wall construction ($2 \times 4$ studs plus $\frac{1}{2}$ in. sheet rock on both sides), which would be most economical, to a fully cased jamb (Fig. 7.1A). The latter will generally exceed the maximum standard widths of materials or units available, and will have to be custom fabricated, resulting in considerable additional cost.

The additional wall thickness also imposes limitations to the door swing unless the frame is located at the extreme edge of the opening which will then allow a full 180° door swing. If not located at the extreme edge, the door swing will be limited to 90° by the wall return at the opening.

The second determination is the type of frame anchor to be used. Although some types of anchor devices may be installed after construction of the wall, the most secure and economical must be installed as the wall is constructed. Doors offer more problems than windows in that the vibration is severe, tending to loosen conventional type anchors, such as lag and shield-metal anchors.

If a full "gringo" block anchor (wood adobe) is laid in the wall as it is constructed, the finished frame may be at any position with respect to the door location in the wall, as it offers a full fastening surface for the entire width of the wall. (Fig. 7.1B). In the case of rammed earth, the wooden "T" anchor may be smaller, and the location must be determined in advance (Fig. 7.1C).

Another option that may be employed is the use of a rough frame which will be concealed by additional trim millwork or plaster. The use of a rough frame may offer more flexibility in accurately constructing the door-frame opening for plumb and square, and will also make placement of the bricks or rammed wall more economical (Fig. 7.2).

**DOOR HEADS**   The detailing of door heads must follow patterns compatible with the jamb detail, and will require additional appearance considerations as well (Fig. 7.3). The lintel may be full wall thickness or less, covered with wood millwork trim, left exposed as solid wood timbers or another material, or faced with wood or masonry (Fig. 7.4).

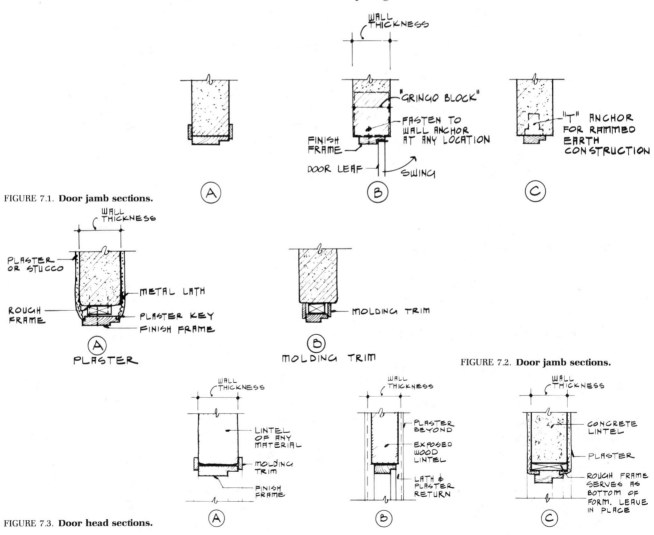

FIGURE 7.1. **Door jamb sections.**

FIGURE 7.2. **Door jamb sections.**

FIGURE 7.3. **Door head sections.**

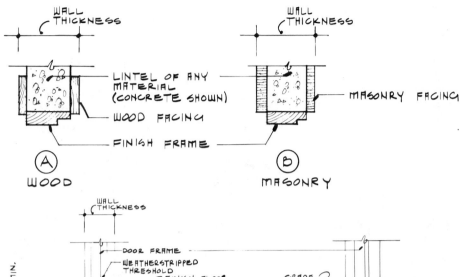

FIGURE 7.4. **Alternate door head details.**

FIGURE 7.5. **Door sills.**

## DOOR SILLS

Door sills can be constructed of any compatible material. For interior doors, the finish floor material will be adequate (Fig. 7.5A). For exterior doors, a waterproof sill should be incorporated, with a drainage slope provided to carry any rainwater away from, instead of into, the building (Fig. 7.5B). A threshold and weatherstripping should also be provided. It is simplest to make all door measurements from the finish floor grade, and trim the door after installation, to accommodate the threshold. Any wood members, rough or finish frames, should not go below the finish floor when it is of brick or concrete, thereby avoiding damp or dry rot and insect damage.

## WINDOW JAMBS

Many of the detailing features of doors in earth walls apply to windows as well. Since the major enemy of the earth wall is water, additional steps to prevent water infiltration are important. Most manufactures of windows do not make provision for the additional wall thickness, so the location of the window in the wall must be carefully determined.

The anchorage of the window frames in the wall is not as critical as in the case of doors, as there is little or no vibration to deal with. A minimum of anchor points will be adequate, seldom more than two per jamb, except in the case of very tall windows. A rough frame may be used in the design, for the same considerations detailed in door frames (Fig. 7.6).

## WINDOW HEADS

Window head detailing is similar to that of door heads, except that where most exterior doors are sheltered from the weather by some sort of porch or canopy, windows may not be. Heavy driving rains may penetrate the window-head trim or run back along horizontal members if detailing does not prevent this, either with a drip edge or kerf-cut drip groove (Fig. 7.7).

[115]

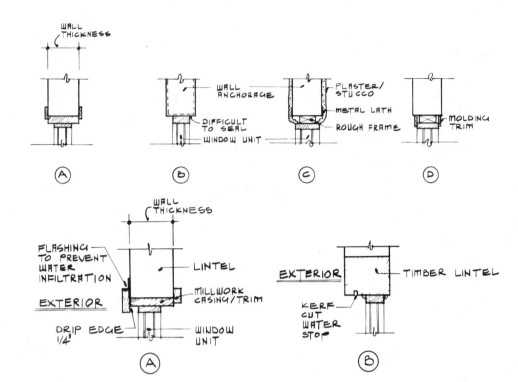

FIGURE 7.6. **Window jambs.**

FIGURE 7.7. **Window heads.**

**WINDOW SILLS**   Manufactured window units usually incorporate a sloping drip sill on the exterior so the unit must be placed to the outside of the wall and/or provided with a sill extension. The interior will also be subject to moisture from open windows or condensation accumulation, as well as physical abuse from objects, such as flower pots, placed on the window sills. A sturdy water-proof sill material is desirable. The use of plaster for sills or sill flashing is usually not satisfactory (Fig. 7.8).

Proper design of window sills provides a physical barrier to stop water flow to the inside, and does not depend on caulking alone, with a positive drainage slope and drip edge to prevent run-back on horizontal members (Fig. 7.9).

**CUSTOM OR JOB-FABRICATED UNITS**   Window and door manufacturers are generally aware of all the ramifications of water and moisture flow control, and deal with these in the design of their standard units. When designing special or custom units, some of the basic requirements may be overlooked. This is, perhaps, even more likely in job-fabricated items. Special care must be taken to incorporate basic principles into the design.

**FASTENING ANCHORS FOR EXISTING WALLS**   While it is best to anticipate anchorage requirements and install anchors as the wall is built, the occasion will arise where it is necessary to provide nail or screw anchors in existing walls for the installation of cabinets or other heavy items. A wooden plug may be cemented in place, but may loosen when the wood dries.

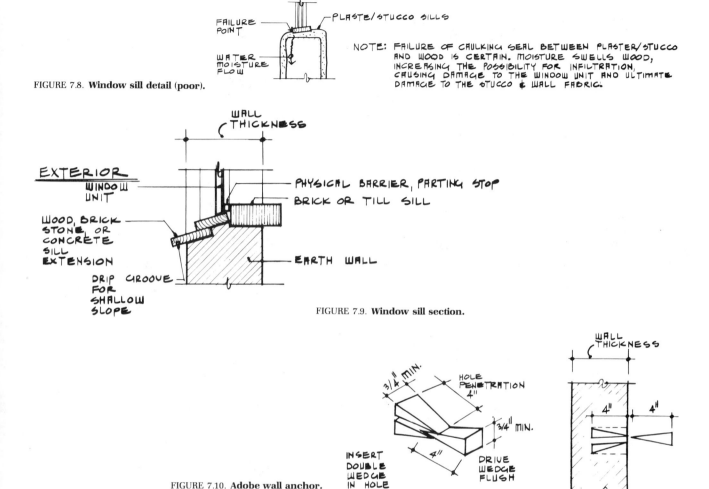

FIGURE 7.8. **Window sill detail (poor).**

NOTE: FAILURE OF CHULKING SEAL BETWEEN PLASTER/STUCCO AND WOOD IS CERTAIN. MOISTURE SWELLS WOOD, INCREASING THE POSSIBILITY FOR INFILTRATION, CAUSING DAMAGE TO THE WINDOW UNIT AND ULTIMATE DAMAGE TO THE STUCCO & WALL FABRIC.

FIGURE 7.9. **Window sill section.**

FIGURE 7.10. **Adobe wall anchor.**

The most successful anchor is a triple wedge made of wood. A square hole is cut in the wall to the same dimension as the anchor, to the anchor depth. Four inches (10 cm) is sufficient (Fig. 7.10). A short piece of square steel tubing, sharpened on one end, is the most practical form of drill. The triple-wedge anchor is then driven into the wall until it is flush with the surface, spreading the wedges at the back of the hole. This form of anchor may be purchased, or may be built on the job with scrap material.

**SUMMARY**

1. Water flow and moisture control are of primary importance in earth wall designing and detailing.

2. Standard manufactured door and window units are more likely to be adequately detailed than custom- or job-fabricated items, but must be additionally detailed to deal with extra wall thickness.

3. Selection of materials must be carefully considered, as the movement (twisting of uncured wood or timber) or failure of one element may generate other problems or failures not anticipated.

[**117**]

## chapter eight

# Earth Wall Finishes

The surface of earth walls, both interior and exterior, is somewhat more fragile, although not as vulnerable as popularly believed. The fragility is mainly cosmetic and not structural. Initial treatment of the surface can take two basic approaches, each with its own advantages and disadvantages. Natural earth finishes can be achieved simply and at moderate cost. This lower initial cost may be offset by higher maintenance costs due to the frequency of the need for cosmetic treatment, but that is also simple and inexpensive. More permanent, longer-wearing waterproof-type surfaces are more expensive initially, and also may create costly long-term maintenance problems. Waterproof surfaces, such as cement stucco, contain and trap moisture, while naturally surfaced earth walls will absorb and give off air borne moisture, allowing the wall to breathe. Mud plaster will also show the occurance of moisture in the wall, from other sources.

**NATURAL MUD SURFACES**

Natural mud wall surfaces offer many advantages. A commonly held belief is that a heavy rain will severely erode and damage the surface of an unprotected mud wall. The clay content inherent in the brick will resist wetting, except at the surface. Natural erosion rates for vertical surfaces have been determined to be approximately 1 in. (2.5 cm) in 20 years. The existence of many abandoned mud wall ruins also attests to this (Fig. 8.1).

A typical example of this is a ranch house in southern Arizona, which was unoccupied and neglected, with no maintenance for a period of 26 years. Average rainfall for the area is approximately 25 in./year. The bricks for the walls were made from basement excavation soils at the site and were pro-

FIGURE 8.1. **Casa Grande national monument, Casa Grande, Arizona 1976 (ca. 1000 A.D.). These mud walls were unprotected for many centuries until a weather shelter was built by the National Park Service in 1932.**

FIGURE 8.2. Lone Mountain ranch headquarters, Sonoita, Arizona. 1975. This ranch home has not been maintained for more than 26 years. (a) The mud plaster was flush with the concrete foundation wall when it was built, and the erosion measures less than 1 in. (b) Erosion could also be measured at the window frames, where cement plaster was used to flash between the windows and the walls.

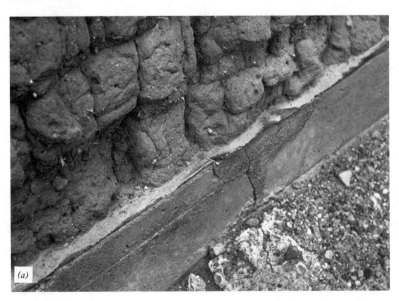

tected at the top with a roof overhang of approximately 2 ft (61 cm). Resultant erosion was measured at the foundation wall and window flashings (Fig. 8.2a,b). One location had more severe erosion due to a leaky downspout which concentrated the water flow (Fig. 8.3).

If the earth material (adobe bricks or rammed earth) has a reasonable amount of clay content (10–20%), the surface will resist erosion from ambient rainfall to some degree. If the clay content is too low, and the surface material sandy, wind driven rain can cause severe erosion. Rain erosion may tend to be more pronounced on the side of the building that is exposed to prevailing wind and storm patterns.

If the masonry texture of the wall is to be exposed, more care must be exercised in the laying of the wall, maintaining level brick courses and carefully filling the joints. The texture can range from a *struck* finish, where mud mortar joints are trimmed with a trowel, to *raked* mortar joints, where each brick is clearly defined. In either case, additional detailing will be required at

**NATURAL TEXTURED BRICK WALLS**

FIGURE 8.3. **Lone Mountain ranch headquarters, cont. Erosion was accelerated at the point where a roof-drain downspout had rusted out. The concrete bond beam, which was originally flush with the wall surface, offers an additional reference.**

the juncture of window and door frames and nonsimilar materials such as concrete or wood beams (Fig. 8.4). Additional attention must be paid to wood anchoring devices such as "gringo" blocks (Chapter 7). Simple "gringo" blocks of scrap wood nailed together will be adequate where they are to be covered with plaster. Exposed "gringo' blocks must be carefully planned and detailed. An alternate treatment can be selected, framing openings with a plaster casing (Fig. 8.5).

Decorative detailing of the masonry fabric may also be a viable choice, either in the placement of the brick or as an incised pattern in the walls (Fig. 8.6). The latter may be easily accomplished with a hatchet or chisel, without damaging the integrity of the mud brick wall (Fig. 8.7). Mud is essentially a sculptural material. Projecting cornices of unplastered or unprotected adobe masonry should be avoided, because the low tensile strength of the brick

FIGURE 8.4. **Grisham house, Albuquerque, New Mexico, 1978. Straight door-frame trim must meet irregular adobe brick surface, so it must be scribed, or the gap filled with plaster or caulking. Wood gringo blocks for attaching frames must be of finished wood because they will be exposed. Bruce McHenry photo.**

FIGURE 8.5. **Kinney house, Albuquerque, New Mexico, 1982. The flashing problem between textured adobe walls and straight window jambs was solved by the use of sculptured plaster to make the transition. Bruce McHenry photo.**

FIGURE 8.6. **Palace wall, Iran, 1972. A masonry pattern was built into this wall as it was constructed. Minimal weathering has occurred.**

FIGURE 8.7. **Olson house, Albuquerque, New Mexico, 1976. Wall niches for displaying statuary and art work can be easily cut into earth walls.**

makes isolated projections particularly subject to damage. Wood is compatible with mud, and once the final pointing up and surfacing of mud surfaces adjacent to exposed wood surfaces has been accomplished, it will be stable and require little further care.

## MUD PLASTER

Mud plaster is a traditional treatment for mud brick walls. It is normally applied in two coats, both for exterior and interior surfaces. The initial coat does not require the application of galvanized mesh or stucco netting for interior or exterior. The first coat might be compared with the "brown" coat in conventional plaster practice. The application of an anchor or "scratch" coat is omitted. The initial mud plaster coat is best reinforced with a small quantity of straw or fibrous material. This might be compared with fibered gypsum plaster used for the brown coat of interior plaster finishes. The reason for the fibered material is twofold. First, it will allow the use of a higher percentage of clay (20–25%) in the mud plaster mix, and second, it will reinforce it, making possible the application of thicker coats for leveling the surface, where necessary. The higher clay content may cause shrinkage cracks on drying, the size and severity of the cracks will be proportionate to the clay content and the thickness of the plaster. If the clay content is too high, the shrinkage on drying may also result in a poor bond to the mud brick surface.

The final or finish coat is made up of screened, fine material, also with a moderately high clay content, and is applied as thinly as possible to achieve full coverage. If small shrinkage cracks appear in the final coat, these may be easily dealt with by dampening the surface, which recreates the plasticity of the mud so that it can be retroweled or refloated for a smooth finish. Mud plaster surfaces will take a hard, firm set, very similar in texture and hardness to conventional plaster, but which is not totally waterproof as is conventional plaster. It may be replastered or refloated as many times as is necessary. This feature is also useful in the repairing and patching of damaged surfaces.

**FINISHES**      The final finish of mud plaster can assume the same approximate finish as used in conventional plaster. Textured, where the final surface is troweled roughly, creating a rough surface, troweled completely smooth, making a

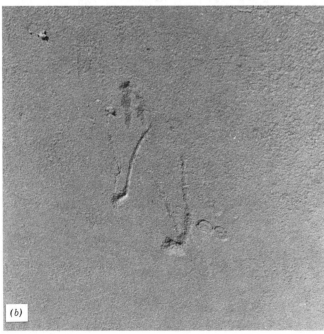

FIGURE 8.8. **YWCA summer camp building, Tijeras, New Mexico, 1982.** (*a*) **This is a mud plastered adobe wall, with a floated sand finish. Resurfacing was done in 1979. The only sign of wear or erosion are scratches caused by vandalism. A cement stucco patch only 1 year old is loose and unsightly. Application of mud and a sponge rubber float could have created a surface that blended.** (*b*) **A close look shows the sand grains from the float finish, with abrasion damage.**

[124]

FIGURE 8.9. **Rancho Las Golandrinas, La Cieniga, New Mexico. Mud plaster reinforced with short pieces of straw erodes slowly in a distinctive pattern.**

hard flat surface, or by floating for a "sand" finish. Conventional sponge rubber floats may be used, or a sheepskin. The sheepskin float will produce a finer, softer finish (Fig. 8.8). Special effects may be created by the addition of other materials to the finish coat such as straw. If this is done, the fibrous material must be chopped into short lengths so as not to protrude from the finished surface. Specially selected wheat or oat straw can impart a shiny, golden surface that reflects the sunlight, creating a pleasing visual effect. This may have given rise to the legend of the Seven Golden Cities of Cibola, which early Spanish explorers of the southwestern United States searched for. The straw material will also reinforce the surface providing some additional protection from rainfall (Fig. 8.9).

**LATHING FOR MUD PLASTER**

The lathing necessary in preparation for the application of mud plaster is minimal. In conventional plasters, all wood surfaces must be waterproofed with asphalt felt, and reinforced with metal lath. As the mud plaster and wood materials in the earth wall seem to be compatible and have about the same coefficients of expansion, the waterproofing and lathing is not required. One location that should be reinforced with metal lath is at door jambs. The vibrations of a door closing tend to crack and separate the plaster from the door jamb. Any location that will be subject to vibration, or which has only a thin layer of mud plaster over a dissimilar material, should be reinforced with metal lath.

**STABILIZED MUD PLASTER**

Mud plaster may be stabilized with the same waterproofing used for the stabilization of mud bricks, and in approximately the same percentage. Asphalt emulsion is the most economical and the most widely used. Portland cement added to the mud plaster (soil cement) is also effective, but when enough cement is added to be effective (15% in most cases) the cost may approach or exceed that of conventional plaster. A long-term effect sometimes found in soil cement, particularly if inadequate quantities of portland cement are used, is one of irregular erosion. If the added cement is not adequately mixed, some areas (sometimes small lumps of soil or clay) may erode completely, leaving a "swiss cheese" type of surface, full of small holes. It is also necessary to use conventional lathing techniques, stucco net and metal lath, to reinforce the surface and prevent spalling and cracking.

A problem inherent in stabilized mud plaster is one of separation. Unstabilized mud plaster will absorb and release moisture at a different rate than stabilized material, and this will cause a separation at the point where they meet. There is often a bonding problem, similar to patches in concrete or stucco. Asphalt emulsion stabilized plasters may be more effective in this regard, particularly if the surface is fresh and has not had a chance to oxidize. Asphalt stabilized surfaces initially are a darker color than natural mud. Time and exposure to sunlight will ultimately fade this surface to the lighter color of natural mud. This may be an indication of evaporation or oxidation of the asphalt, leaving a dusty friable surface to which new layers of material may not adhere. One procedure to reactivate and consolidate the surface is to add a light primary coat of asphalt compatible (petroleum-based) coating prior to the application of the new asphalt stabilized plaster.

## CEMENT STUCCO FOR EXTERIOR WALLS

The most common weatherproofing treatment for earth walls, in the United States at least, is cement stucco. In many other nations, mud plaster is the accepted standard. Cement stucco will provide a weatherproof exterior surface that offers a wide range of colors and textures. It is a durable surface that if properly applied should have a maintenance free life of 10–15 years or more. The stucco surface will remain intact for many years beyond that, although it may develop cracks and need resurfacing. It is not without its drawbacks however. The principal one is that it has a different coefficient of expansion than adobe, and allows little moisture migration through the surface. Although this might seem desirable, it will ultimately lead to a separation from the earth surface, and may conceal water erosion problems from other sources such as leaky roofs, pipes, and flashings, which may have severely damaged the wall fabric. The damage may not be apparent until serious structural problems or collapse occurs. A less serious problem would be the cracking of the surface coat from expansion or settlement, which may allow additional quantities of water to enter the wall. Due to the latter effect, it is most desirable that some sort of reinforcing be provided, such as stucco netting. If this is not done, a series of cracks may interconnect, allowing a large section of the protective stucco to spall off the wall (Fig. 8.10).

## LATHING

The basic lathing material for exterior cement stucco is a hex mesh of galvanized wire. Several wire weights and sizes are available. The most common is "stucco netting," 17 gauge galvanized wire with a hexagonal pattern

FIGURE 8.10. **Cement stucco without stucco netting, Algodones, New Mexico, 1978. If cracks connect, large patches of cement stucco may spall off when not reinforced with stucco netting.**

of $1\frac{1}{2}$ in. (4 cm). Another common size is a 20 gauge 1 in. (2.5 cm) hex pattern, more commonly referred to as "chicken wire" or poultry netting. The heavier mesh (17 gauge) may be the most desirable, but is more costly for both material and application. It is available both in flat or "self-furring" patterns, the latter being designed primarily for use over flat insulation boards, the furring ridges holding the wire away from the wall, which allows the stucco to flow behind it, encasing it completely. If the "self-furring" feature is not present, it is customary to use "furring nails" with a fiber washer to hold the stucco net away from flat surfaces. The furring feature is nonessential to its application over adobe bricks however, as the surface will normally be irregular enough to allow the stucco to encapsulate the mesh. For the flat surfaces found in most rammed earth walls, furred out stucco netting is necessary. It is not necessary to apply asphalt felt or building paper on earth walls as is the common practice when lathing over frame construction. The stucco net should be stretched tightly and attached to the earth wall with nails of sufficient length to securely attach the wire. If the fasteners must penetrate insulation applied to the exterior of the wall as well, they must have additional length. Fasteners should have a minimum spacing of 18 in. (46 cm), and some building codes in the United States require closer spacing. The fasteners are best attached to the wire netting by twisting the netting around the wire as it is stretched and nailed. End and side laps of netting should be a minimum of 6 in. (15 cm) (Fig. 8.11). Historical applications without stucco net used large (16 d) nails driven into the wall 12 in. (30 cm) o.c. The nails were left projecting approximately 2 in. (5 cm). This was followed by a scratch coat of cement plaster 2–4 in. (5–10 cm) thick, a costly procedure today.

The corners of door and window frames should be additionally reinforced with metal lath to prevent cracking and spalling (Fig. 8.12).

FIGURE 8.11. **Stucco netting. Stucco netting is nailed directly to the earth walls to reinforce the stucco. Asphalt felt waterproofs the wood lintel which is to be stuccoed as well.**

FIGURE 8.12. **Metal lath trim at windows. Wood surfaces to be covered with plaster or stucco must be waterproofed and reinforced with metal lath at the corners of openings.**

## ANCHOR OR SCRATCH COAT

The cement stucco should be applied in three coats, the first of which is the anchor or scratch coat. The wall may be dampened slightly before application, but excess moisture may soften the wall surface, resulting in possible sloughing of the new material. It is not industry practice to dampen the earth wall prior to the application of the scratch coat. The scratch coat should be strong, relatively rich in cement, and low in lime, to securely enclose the stucco net reinforcing. This coating should have an average thickness of $\frac{5}{8}$ in. (1.5 cm). The mixture proportions by volume are:

6 parts sand
1 part portland cement (type 1 or 2)
$\frac{1}{2}$ part lime

[**128**]

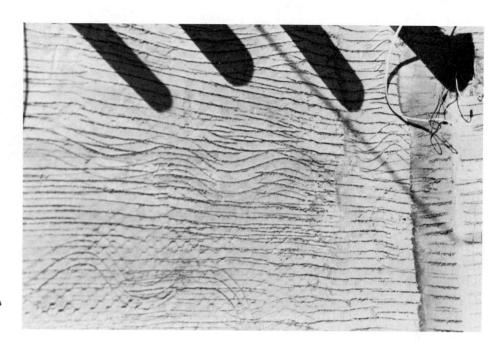

FIGURE 8.13. **Scratch coat. The stucco is not visible under the scratch coat. Horizontal scratches and swirls give tooth for the next coat. Bruce McHenry photo.**

The surface is normally scratched with a toothed strike before setting (Fig. 8.13) to provide grooves for attachment of the second layer, the brown coat. The rich cement coat will often have shrinkage cracks, which are acceptable as they will be filled and covered by following coats. It should be cured by daily applications of water for a period of 7 days. If stucco dries too rapidly it will be soft and crumbly. This condition can be rectified by additional applications of water.

## BROWN COAT

The brown coat is a leveling and shaping coat used to smooth out irregularities in the wall surface, or to create special effects. The volume of material that may be required dictates that the mixture be as economical as possible. The strength requirements are less than for the scratch coat, so that less cement is permissible. The mixture proportions by volume are:

10 parts sand
1 part portland cement (type 1 or 2)
$\frac{1}{2}$ part lime

This mixture results in a sandy rather than gray cement appearance, hence the term "brown" coat. The wall should be dampened with water before application of the brown coat. Two methods are acceptable for its application. The first requires a full curing of the scratch coat, which must have adequate scratch grooves, and is applied a week or more after the initial scratch coat. The second method is called the "double-back", where the brown coat is applied within an hour or so of the scratch coat. If this method

FIGURE 8.14. (a) Texture coat. After initial covering with color, additional stucco is "dashed" on and the trowel allowed to skip. (b) Special trowel texture. Additional stucco applied with a trowel to create special effects or textures. Bruce McHenry photos.

is used, heavy scratching is not required, and the brown coat is applied after the scratch coat has taken an initial set, but is not cured. The application of a cementitious layer to a "green" (unset) previous layer helps insure its adhesion. The final surface of the brown coat should be floated smooth with a sponge rubber float to reduce the quantities of color coat required. This surface should be cured by daily applications of water as specified for the scratch coat, prior to application of the color coat.

**COLOR COAT**

The color coat material is expensive, therefore it should be used as sparingly and in a layer as thin as possible to insure uniform color. Its thickness is normally as thin as can be applied, about $\frac{1}{16}$ in. (3 mm). It is almost like paint and adds no strength to the surface. Proper smoothing and void filling with the brown coat will result in less material being required for the color coat.

The color coat is applied with a trowel (or brush) and textured as desired, or floated smooth for a "sand" finish. The float finish will bring sand particles to the surface, producing a uniformly smooth sandy texture (Fig. 8.8a,b). Trowel textures may be applied, allowing the trowel to skip, chatter, or provide special swirl effects (Fig. 8.14). In some instances the stucco surface may be scored or painted to simulate another material such as concrete block or brick (Fig. 8.15).

FIGURE 8.15. **Simulated block finish. The final stucco coat is scored to simulate the appearance of concrete block. The final thin coating in this photo is spalling off.**

**INTERIOR GYPSUM PLASTER**

Interior plaster has many of the same features and details of exterior stucco but is simpler. Water and ambient moisture problems are considerably less, and the plaster will not usually separate from the earth wall as it does on exterior stuccoed surfaces.

**LATHING**

Lathing is minimal, interior adobe brick walls normally requiring none. Rammed earth walls may be too smooth to offer a good tooth for the bonding of the plaster, so it is desirable that the surfaces to be plastered are scratched before curing, pecked (chipped or roughened) to provide a mechanical tooth, or covered with stucco netting held away from the surface.

Any wood surfaces that are to be plastered with cement, lime, or gypsum plasters must be waterproofed with asphalt felt, and the surface must be reinforced with metal lath. Vertical and horizontal corners where plaster meets finished wood surfaces (i.e. window and door frames) must also be waterproofed and reinforced with metal lath. Inside corners that join dissimilar materials must also be lathed. If it is desirable to maintain sharp outside corners or other straight lines, it is best to use a preformed lath corner or plaster ground. These are installed at the corners and edges prior to plastering, so the plaster can be shaped to a preformed lath corner or edge.

It it also desirable for finished wood-surface edges to be provided with a "plaster key" or rabbet to additionally secure the plaster at that point (Fig. 8.16).

FIGURE 8.16. **Plaster key. Door and window frames may be rabbetted at the corners to attach metal lath reinforcing more securely.**

The scratch coat is normally omitted on interior plastered walls. The brown coat is made up of fibered gypsum plaster, fortified with lime, and applied with an average thickness of $\frac{3}{4}$ in. (2 cm). The mixture proportions by volume are:

**BROWN COAT**

1 part fibered gypsum plaster
5 parts sand

If gypsum plaster is not available, sand/lime/cement plasters may be used in the same manner described for exterior stucco, but omitting the scratch coat and stucco net.

The finish coat for interiors offers two choices, either a smooth putty coat or one of rougher texture. The smooth coat is most desirable, as it will be less subject to the collection of dust and will offer a more pleasing appearance. It is made up of lime putty mixed with guaging plaster (plaster of paris), and is available as a manufactured material. It is normally applied in as thin a layer as possible, but must be thicker than the exterior color coat. Average thickness will be $\frac{1}{8}$ in. (3–4 mm). The mixture proportions by volume are:

**FINISH COAT**

1 part lime or finish plaster
2 parts sand

Another vernacular solution that has been used for centuries is the local manufacture of lime and gypsum for use as plaster, where manufactured materials are unavailable or unaffordable.

Prepare quicklime from limestone in a kiln as detailed in chapter four. Slake this in water for as long as possible, preparing a lime putty of trowelable consistency. Mix this with sand and screened earth for a trowelable plaster mix and apply it to the earth surface, trowelling it smooth or floating for a sand finish. The mix proportions by volume are:

**Lime Sand Plaster**

1 part lime putty
5 parts sand (washed)
1 part screened earth

Gypsum plaster is sometimes called "Yeso" in the Spanish Southwest of the United States. Gypsum is ground to as fine a powder as possible, heated (calcined) to drive off water content, and mixed with sand and water to form a plaster paste that can be trowelled on the wall. If the powder is heated sufficiently it will become plaster of paris and, if not, will be partly calcined, which will work as well but have a shorter setting time (chapter five).

**Gypsum Plaster**

**PAINTS AND SEALERS**

**Exteriors**

Exterior stucco surfaces should not be painted with standard manufactured paints. Most modern paints of oil or synthetic plastic base tend to form a moisture barrier. While this might seem desirable, the moisture migration that will occur causes a loosening of the paint coating from the surface causing cracks and peeling. If this occurs, additional coats of paint will be difficult to apply, may not adhere properly, and will not have a long life. In cases of the severe peeling of previously applied paint, it may be necessary to remove it by sandblasting, or other mechanical means, to provide a fresh cement surface to which new cement coatings will adhere. In some extreme cases it may be necessary to remove the existing stucco entirely or to repeat the entire stucco net and three coat stucco process.

Exterior earth surfaces are best left untreated. They will accept paint, but the bond between earth and paint is fragile and will not hold for any period of time. Moisture is the villain that softens any earth surface. Life may be increased by the priming or sizing of the surface prior to application of paint, and by the installation of wide roof overhangs on the structure. Some heavy paints designed for masonry have had some limited success, but when the coating begins to fail the coating that is still in place must be removed before a new smooth finish can be applied.

A number of chemical compounds have been investigated for application to existing earth surfaces, particularly in the case of historic monuments. Surface coatings generally fail for the reasons stated earlier. Other trials have been made using penetrating sealers which may consolidate the surface to a depth of $\frac{1}{4}$ in. (6 mm) or more. Some of these seemed initially successful, but in most cases failed after a few years, the entire consolidated surface sloughing off. Since the natural erosion rate may be as little as 1 in. (2.5 cm) in 20 years, the stabilization may actually increase the net erosion effect rather than slow it down.

**Interior**

Interior earth surfaces can be sealed and painted more successfully than exterior surfaces. The lack of ambient moisture sources reduces the moisture penetration and its subsequent damage.

The natural (untreated) earth wall surface will continue to dust and have a tendency to rub off on clothing and furnishings. This may be prevented by a number of sealing compounds, such as silicones and other plastic compounds that act as sizing agents, which consolidate the surface to some degree. Simple materials such as oil base varnishes and resinous liquids can be used effectively in a very diluted state. If paint is to be used, such as latex, the wall should be sealed or sized prior to painting to insure paint coverage. For example, Latex-type paints, which are more expensive than many sealing compounds, will not color the wall evenly and will require a number of coats, unless the surface has first been sealed.

Whitewash, a common low-cost paint, can be prepared as a wall color by mixing equal parts of lime and white cement, adding 1 lb of sodium chloride (common salt) per 100 lbs of lime, and mixing with water to make a liquid of paint consistency which can be applied to earth walls or wood surfaces.

In most geographic areas, natural soil deposits containing colored clays **Earth Colors** can be found. These soils mixed with water can be effectively used to stain and color both earth and wood surfaces. The colored clay pigment, after all, is the basic coloring agent for paints. If used in its natural state, with water as a diluting agent, the clay pigment will bond readily to the earth wall surfaces, and wood surfaces as well. In one instance, the National Park Service used such a treatment to modify and tone down the stark white color of new lime/sand plaster repairs to an old mission.

1. Examine the need for additional wall treatment prior to selection of meth-**SUMMARY** ods and materials. Untreated walls are the most effective, least expensive, and will generate fewer long-term maintenance problems.
2. Examine the qualities and claims of manufactured paints and coatings before committing a project to their extensive use. It may take a period of several years to determine the long-term effectiveness, and other, perhaps, undesirable side effects.

*chapter nine*
# Foundations

Foundations for earth wall construction have basically the same requirements as other foundations. Earth walls generally weigh more than conventional walls, and a factor to consider is the need for adequate strength for the additional weight of the wall. Climatic factors and subsoil conditions must also be evaluated as with any other foundation.

Historically, foundations for earth walls have ranged from none to extremely conservative. An examination of historic structures of great age would indicate that the foundation design that was used was based on the technical knowledge of the builder, the importance of the projected life of the building, and the budget. Earth walls appear to have a certain resilience not found in more conventional materials, so the foundation may be of less importance. There are many extant examples of large strucures with no formal foundations at all, at least as we think of them today. A number of historic churches in New Mexico and Arizona have foundations made of adobe bricks, sometimes with a veneer of stone on the exterior. It is also suspected that the stone veneer may have been a later addition to correct basal erosion problems, and was applied as a repair rather than a part of the original design. In some cases, a rubble-stone foundation wall was built, rising a short distance above the adjacent ground level. In one case in Iran, foundations were reportedly excavated 40 ft to the bedrock. Both extremes are probably undesirable. In the former it was not wise, and in the latter unnecessarily costly. Common examples of historic foundations that have been used are shown in Fig. 9.1. In some developing countries, lime is mixed with dampened soil for compaction.

Current practice, accepted by most codes, uses concrete (Fig. 9.2). Concrete footings reinforced with steel are required by most codes. If this is done, the footing should be designed as a grade beam which will support the

**REQUIREMENTS**

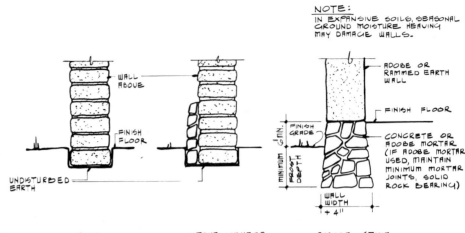

FIGURE 9.1. **Historic adobe foundations.**

weight of the structure imposed on it. A list of typical wall weights is given on Table 9.1. Roof and floor loads are not included, but are relatively unimportant by comparison with the wall weight.

**GRAVEL FOUNDATIONS**   The diversity of successful foundations found in many old adobe buildings has given rise to the possibility of a rediscovered concept in foundations. A number of trial installations have proven successful. This system uses compacted sand/gravel foundations (Fig. 9.2f). A foundation trench is exca-

TABLE 9.1
**Foundation Loading for Adobe Walls (pounds per lineal foot)**

| Wall height (ft) | Wall thickness | | | | | | | | | | psi at bottom of wall |
|---|---|---|---|---|---|---|---|---|---|---|---|
| | 4 in. | 8 in. | 10 in. | 12 in. | 14 in. | 16 in. | 18 in. | 20 in. | 22 in. | 24 in. | |
| 20 | 720 | 1440 | 1800 | 2160 | 2520 | 2880 | 3240 | 3600 | 3960 | 4320 | 15.00 |
| 19 | 684 | 1368 | 1710 | 2052 | 2394 | 2736 | 3078 | 3420 | 3762 | 4104 | 14.25 |
| 18 | 648 | 1296 | 1620 | 1944 | 2268 | 2592 | 2916 | 3240 | 3564 | 3888 | 13.50 |
| 17 | 612 | 1224 | 1530 | 1836 | 2142 | 2448 | 2754 | 3060 | 3366 | 3672 | 12.75 |
| 16 | 576 | 1152 | 1440 | 1728 | 2016 | 2304 | 2592 | 2880 | 3168 | 3456 | 12.00 |
| 15 | 540 | 1080 | 1350 | 1620 | 1890 | 2160 | 2430 | 2700 | 2970 | 3240 | 11.25 |
| 14 | 504 | 1008 | 1260 | 1512 | 1764 | 2016 | 2268 | 2520 | 2772 | 3024 | 10.50 |
| 13 | 468 | 936 | 1170 | 1404 | 1638 | 1872 | 2106 | 2340 | 2574 | 2808 | 9.75 |
| 12 | 432 | 864 | 1080 | 1296 | 1512 | 1728 | 1944 | 2160 | 2376 | 2592 | 9.00 |
| 11 | 396 | 792 | 990 | 1188 | 1386 | 1548 | 1782 | 1980 | 2178 | 2376 | 8.25 |
| 10 | 360 | 720 | 900 | 1080 | 1260 | 1440 | 1620 | 1800 | 1980 | 2160 | 7.50 |
| 9 | 324 | 648 | 810 | 972 | 1134 | 1296 | 1458 | 1620 | 1782 | 1944 | 6.75 |
| 8 | 288 | 576 | 720 | 864 | 1008 | 1152 | 1296 | 1440 | 1584 | 1728 | 6.00 |
| 7 | 252 | 504 | 630 | 756 | 882 | 1008 | 1134 | 1260 | 1386 | 1512 | 5.25 |
| 6 | 216 | 432 | 540 | 648 | 756 | 864 | 972 | 1080 | 1188 | 1296 | 4.50 |
| 5 | 180 | 360 | 450 | 540 | 630 | 720 | 810 | 900 | 990 | 1080 | 3.75 |
| 4 | 144 | 288 | 360 | 432 | 504 | 576 | 648 | 720 | 792 | 864 | 3.00 |
| 3 | 108 | 216 | 270 | 324 | 378 | 432 | 486 | 540 | 594 | 648 | 2.25 |
| 2 | 72 | 144 | 180 | 216 | 252 | 288 | 324 | 360 | 396 | 432 | 1.50 |
| 1 | 36 | 72 | 90 | 108 | 126 | 144 | 162 | 180 | 198 | 216 | 0.75 |

*Note:* This table is based on a weight of 108 lb/ft³. Actual weights may vary ±15%.

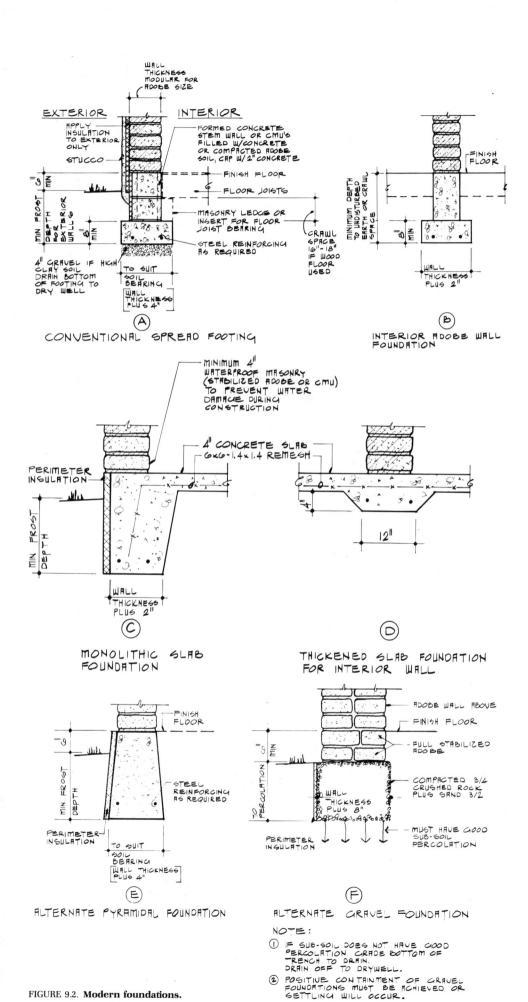

FIGURE 9.2. **Modern foundations.**

vated and filled with a mixture of 2 parts sand to 3 parts gravel. This is commonly known as the "base course" in highway construction.

The compressive strength of gravel is normally adequate to support anticipated loads. Since it has high percolation, and if the soil substrate has adequate percolation, there is no opportunity for water buildup, thus avoiding frost heaving, a major cause of damage in masonry buildings. This type of foundation is inexpensive and could be a factor in reducing construction costs. A note of caution is advised however for a careful investigation of the soil substrate. If the substrate is of high clay content, it could conceivably trap and hold any water accumulation in the trench, creating an unstable soil base and introducing the possibility of frost heaving. This can be avoided however, by grading the trench bottom for drainage, and draining the moisture off to a gravel drain to a more percolable level.

A number of successful demonstrations have been constructed in the Albuquerque, New Mexico area. The McHenry house, Corrales, New Mexico (Figs. 2.40–2.46) was built with this system. It is not really a new idea, having been used by Frank Lloyd Wright in the Jacobs House in Middleton, Wisconsin prior to World War II. No cracking, settling, or frost heaving was noted by Dr. Jacobs. Other forms of pressure treated wood/gravel foundations are being marketed nationally as well. Additional formal testing and observation confirming the suitability of this type of system could produce substantial construction cost savings.

Caution is advised at any site with extremely high clay subsoil conditions. Building sites with this condition may be subject to seasonal heaving or subsidence of the ground from expansive types of clay. The introduction of more than normal amounts of moisture from flooding, streams, roof drains, leaky plumbing or landscape watering may cause heaving in certain sections of the structure, or the drying out of the clay from normal levels may cause subsidence of the soil. Where this condition is probable, care should be used in designing the footing so that it will resist or support changes in ground levels. Positive drainage should be incorporated in the foundation design so that soil conditions can remain as stable as possible.

Adobe bricks should not be used in below-grade walls where they may be unsupported on one side. Natural ground moisture will infiltrate the wall, and can reduce the compressive strength of the brick to the point of failure. If the wall is contained on both sides, it will merely act as totally compacted earth.

Foundations for earth walls should be designed with the same consideration as any other type of wall, subject to the special conditions noted above.

## chapter ten

# Floor and Roof Structures

The choice of a floor or roof structural system for use in earth construction differs little from framing systems for conventional construction. Considerations for member strength to deal with dead and live loads remain the same. The primary difference lies in the connections and detailing of the connections bearing on earth wall structures. In some climates, wide eave overhangs may be desirable to give additional protection to earth walls.

**FLOOR SYSTEMS**

Many earth structures utilize solid floors of concrete, masonry, or compacted earth. The primary requirement is one of solid compaction of the substrate to support the final flooring material, and control of moisture and insects through the finished floor. Additionally, the floor system may play a part in the control of moisture migration from natural ground water to the earth walls, as well as furnish additional thermal mass.

**Concrete Floors**

Concrete floors can generally be of medium strength concrete when used as finished flooring. If the concrete is a part of a monolithic floor–foundation system, it should be of structural grade concrete (2500–3000 psi) and reinforced with metal mesh (6 in × 6 in.—10 ga. × 10 ga. welded wire fabric). If reinforcing is not provided, the loads imposed by the weight of the walls may cause settlement and subsequent cracking of the floor surface. In most arid climates, where ground moisture is nominal, the concrete itself will offer a sufficient moisture barrier, and no additional treatment is required. If an additional moisture barrier is required, it may be in the form of plastic sheeting, asphalt felts, or other suitable moisture-proof material. It may be necessary under severe moisture conditions to install a gravel bed under the vapor barrier and slab to additionally resist upward migration of the moisture (Fig. 10.1).

**Earth Floors**   Earth floors are common historically and in areas where minimum cost is necessary. When properly finished and sealed, the surface is reasonably waterproof and the appearance is very similar to that of concrete. The substrate must be solidly compacted, and the earth floor laid as a plaster mixture that can be compacted and troweled smooth in the same manner as plaster. The process is similar to that of mud plaster in many respects. The soil mixture ideally should be only slightly higher in clay content than the material for bricks and plaster, with enough water added to mix thoroughly and provide a trowelable consistency. It is best laid in several thin layers than one massive layer. The clay content may cause shrinkage cracks as it dries, and the thicker layers will cause larger cracks. The cracks may be filled by dampening with water, and then troweled or floated smooth. It may require several treatments to achieve a smooth, crack-free surface.

The surface is then sealed with a waterproofing material. The finished surface will be darkened by most sealers, and should provide a smooth glossy surface, dependent on the quality and quantity of the sealer. The sealing liquid should be thin enough to penetrate, but not allowed to puddle. Oil varnish or other chemical sealants can be used. Animal blood and plant juices are also used in some vernacular applications. If no waterproofing sealer is applied, the surface can be repeatedly reactivated with water and smoothed as it was originally. Unsealed earth floors will have a fragile surface and will be a continual source of dust (Fig. 10.2).

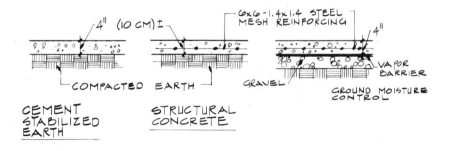

FIGURE 10.1. **Concrete floors.**

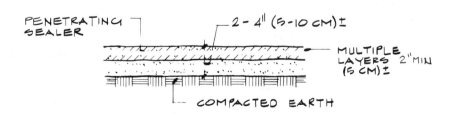

FIGURE 10.2. **Earth floors.**

Fired-brick floors will provide a very satisfactory answer for a finished flooring material. A strong, wear-resistant surface is achieved, and masonry units can be removed easily for repairs to mechanical systems below the floor. It is not necessary, in most instances, to provide a supporting concrete slab *if the brick flooring material is at least 2 in. (6 cm) thick*, and on a fully compacted substrata and sand-leveling bed. The bricks should be placed solidly on a smooth, dry sand bed, 1 in. (3 cm) thick, with fine sand added after laying and cutting in the edges, to fill any irregularities or minor voids between the bricks. After final sanding movement will be minimal, even when concentrated loads are placed on the floor. Top sand fill should not be applied until all cutting, leveling, and adjustments in the floor level are complete. Final sealing with varnish or oil will cement the fine sand particles between the bricks. It is also desirable to treat the substrate with an insecticide and provide a vapor barrier between the substrate and the sand bed. This will prevent any moisture migration from the soil.

Most masonry floors should be finished by sanding or rubbing with a brick, to remove sharp mold cut edges prior to sealing. Mechanical grinding should be avoided, unless the entire surface is done, to avoid partial changes in texture. Sealant will prevent staining from spills. The sealer should be liquid enough to penetrate the surface of the masonry units (Fig. 10.3).

**Masonry Floors**

Glazed tile and prefinished masonry flooring materials are generally too thin to utilize a dry-sand bedding base. A concrete slab of at least 2 in. (5 cm) thickness, or a cement stabilized earth or sand base, may be used. This is often simply done with a weak mixture of portland cement (1 part cement to 8–10 parts damp soil or sand), which will provide solid support for the finish flooring material. If the tile material is installed on an unset (not yet hard) cement stabilized base, the tile should be thoroughly wet and tamped level into the soft base, and additionally secured with a dab of neat cement paste. Grouting of the tile joints should be done as soon as possible to prevent the loosening of the tile from traffic (Fig. 10.4).

**Tile Floors**

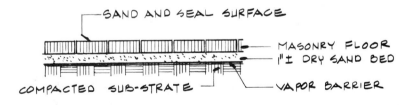

FIGURE 10.3. **Brick floors.**

FIGURE 10.4. **Tile floors.**

**Wood Floors**     Framed wood floors for earth construction are similar to conventional framing systems except for the bearing of structural members on or in the earth wall. The "rim" joist is normally omitted, with adobe bricks filling the space between joists. A crawl or ventilation space must be provided, not only to meet most code requirements, but to prevent moisture and insect damage, and to provide access to mechanical systems. The floor joists must bear on a wall with adequate bearing strength to support concentrated loads and be of sufficient strength to resist anticipated live and dead loads. The joists should bear on the foundation wall or a plate which will provide a more solid bearing surface than the lower compressive strength of earth masonry (Fig. 10.5). Wooden members encased in earth walls are seldom affected by insects (termites) or moisture if a distance of 6 in. (15 cm) is maintained between ground level and wood members (Fig. 10.5B).

**Floor Insulation**     The insulation of solid floors is problematical and will depend on climatic conditions. Earth temperatures are stable below the surface and are approximately 55°F in most parts of the world. The isolation of the earth mass at 55°F as a heat sink may be desirable during the hot season, but may be a detriment during the cool season. The length and severity of the hot and cool seasons must be analysed to determine the cost effectiveness of any insulation to be considered. Any floor insulation of this type should also be impervious to moisture (Fig. 10.6A).

On the other hand, insulation of wood-flooring structures over a ventilated crawl space is effective in any climate where heating requirements are significant. The ventilated space, in effect, becomes an outside space and requires insulation to the same degree as an exterior wall (Fig. 10.6B).

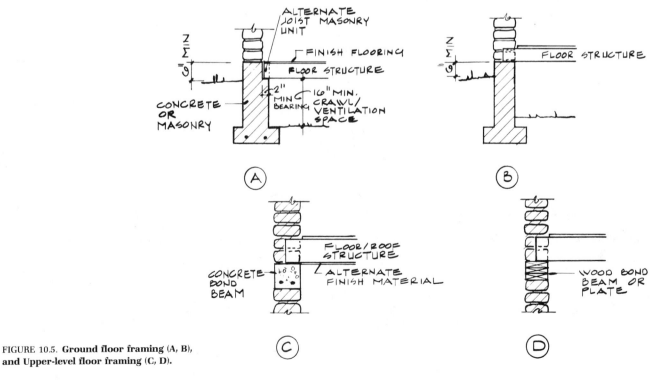

FIGURE 10.5. **Ground floor framing (A, B), and Upper-level floor framing (C, D).**

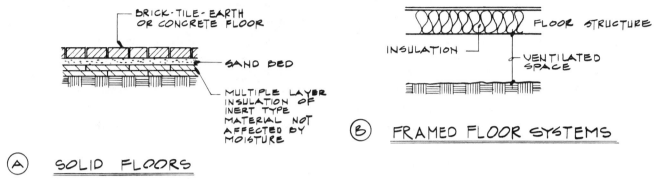

FIGURE 10.6. **Solid floors (A), and framed floor systems (B).**

**ROOF STRUCTURES**

The choice of roof structure will be governed by considerations of architectural style, cost, and availability of materials as in any other selection criteria. The earth walls present more of a problem in anchorage. Most earth structures in vernacular architectural styles in low-rainfall climates are provided with flat or minimum-slope roof structures, without significant overhangs, except perhaps for sun control. Most earth walls do not have continuous vertical reinforcing within the wall, connecting foundations to the bond beam or plate at the top of the wall. The roof structure will depend primarily on weight to anchor the roof structure to the top of the wall. Most flat roof structures should have parapet walls of earth providing additional weight anchorage, and controlling the flow of collected rainwater to specific disposal points (Fig. 10.7A).

If an overhang is used, it will create a moment reaction, increasing wind-uplift forces. When an overhang is present, additional securement and/or weight may be necessary, perhaps most logically provided by a concrete bond beam. Bond-beam anchorage can be extended downward into the wall with additional bolts and plates if necessary (Fig. 10.7B).

If local wind conditions present a possible problem, probable wind uplift forces should be calculated and designed for accordingly.

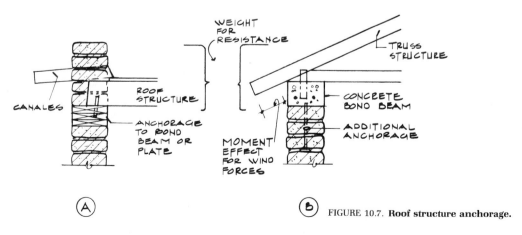

FIGURE 10.7. **Roof structure anchorage.**

**ROOF INSULATION**     Historical solutions for roof insulation, drainage, and waterproofing often made use of earth as the total material. In cases where economic problems prevent the use of more modern, efficient materials, earth can still be used effectively. Its insulation value is minimal unless very thick, although the thermal mass effect will be beneficial. The dead load of such earth roofs will also increase the structural requirements to support it. It must be solidly compacted to be effective (Fig. 10.8).

Modern insulation and roofing materials may be efficiently used, and their selection will be determined by the interior finishes desired. If the roof structure is to be exposed below for decorative purposes (i.e. exposed beams), insulation must be added above the ceiling deck, either in the form of solid roof insulation or in the form of an additional roof structure with decking, providing a cavity space for soft, more economical insulation. If the roof structure is to be concealed, the structure itself may provide a cavity space within, in which economical insulation may be utilized (Fig. 10.9).

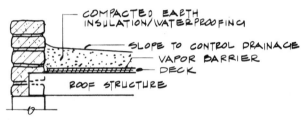

FIGURE 10.8. **Earth roofing.**

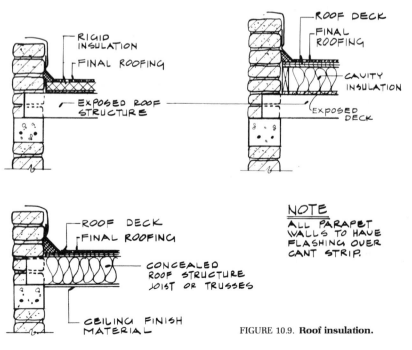

FIGURE 10.9. **Roof insulation.**

In many hostile arid environments, structural wood members may be difficult and expensive to obtain. Evidence of vaulted brick structures has been found as early as 8000 B.C. in the Middle East, where small masonry units were used to create structural roofing systems. Vaults and domes transfer roof loads to a vertical wall. Most are related to and are a form of arch. Often the specific form and shape result from trial-and-error efforts yielding traditional practices that have been used successfully. Various geographic areas have traditional proven forms.

**VAULTS AND DOMES**

The barrel vault is a form of continuous arch. There are two patterns in common use. One uses the major flat side of the masonry unit perpendicular to the span, and the other parallel with it (Fig. 10.10). The parallel form can be erected without any temporary support (centering), with earth mortar, using friction and the adhesive quality of the earth mortar. This type of barrel vault must be started against a backup wall, and the bricks must be laid at a slight angle to increase the friction (Fig. 10.11). The circular form of the vault may be either catenary or hemispherical. The catenary form follows the pattern made by the natural hanging shape of a chain suspended from each end. The use of a chain for pattern layout is suggested as a practical matter. This form will transfer the weight of the vault to a vertical vector force on top of the supporting walls, reducing horizontal thrust, as well as the need for thicker supporting walls. When a hemispherical form is used, the dead load of the vault may create horizontal side-thrust vectors which will require thicker

**Barrel Vaults**

 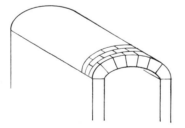

PERPENDICULAR PATTERN     PARALLEL PATTERN

FIGURE 10.10. **Barrel vaults.**

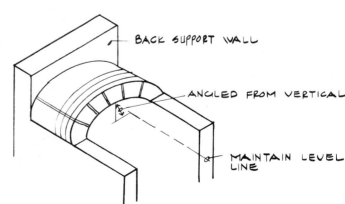

FIGURE 10.11. **Barrel vault construction.**

walls to resist overturning. When a series of barrel vaults are used in parallel combination, the side thrust of one vault will offset the thrust of the adjacent one, eliminating the need for thicker supporting walls except at the ends. Most barrel vaults do not exceed a span of 14 ft (4 m) (Fig. 10.12). Some larger monumental forms are found in Iran, where a catenary form is used, with the spring line starting at ground level.

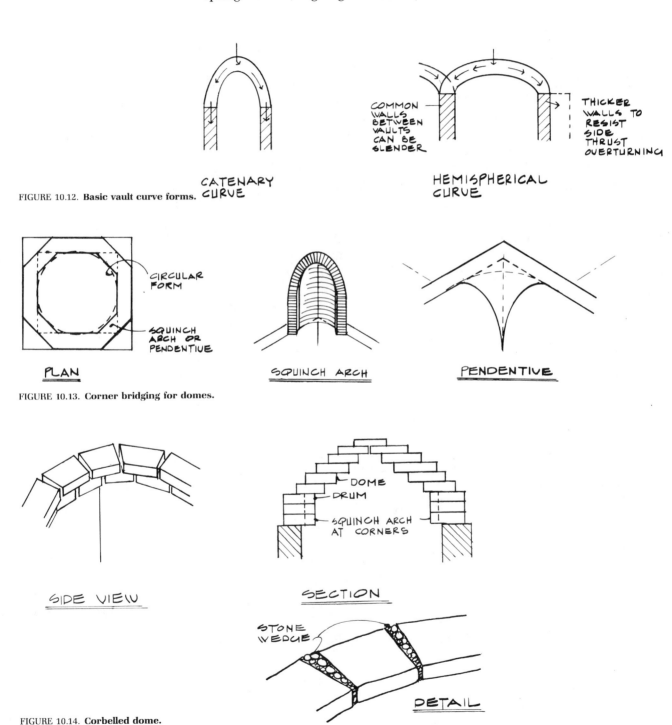

FIGURE 10.12. **Basic vault curve forms.**

CATENARY CURVE

HEMISPHERICAL CURVE

COMMON WALLS BETWEEN VAULTS CAN BE SLENDER

THICKER WALLS TO RESIST SIDE THRUST OVERTURNING

FIGURE 10.13. **Corner bridging for domes.**

CIRCULAR FORM

SQUINCH ARCH OR PENDENTIVE

PLAN

SQUINCH ARCH

PENDENTIVE

FIGURE 10.14. **Corbelled dome.**

SIDE VIEW

SECTION

DOME
DRUM
SQUINCH ARCH AT CORNERS

STONE WEDGE

DETAIL

Domes can be easily employed for roof structures using adobe bricks. The compressive stresses that domes generate are low enough in most instances to be resisted by the compressive strength of earth masonry.

The corners of a rectangular building must first be redesigned, employing either a squinch arch or pendentive structure, to make a transition from square or rectangular to an octagon or a more circular shape. Once the corners have been bridged, they offer support for a circular form (Fig. 10.13). A drum wall may be constructed in a circular vertical form before starting the dome proper.

The earliest form of dome, like the earliest form of arch, was probably done in a corbelled pattern, with each course of brick projecting a measured amount past the course below it. The design potential or corbelled domes is limited and tends to make a cone shape rather than a curve (Figs. 10.14 and 10.15).

Unless the bricks are cut and shaped to fit tightly as required for the circular form, wide mud-mortar joints may result. Until these are dry they will not have adequate strength to resist compressive stresses. They also may further transmit moisture to the bricks themselves, making the structure unsound until it dries. Where thicker mortar joints are necessary, it is common practice to drive stones or waterproof wedges in the mortar joints so that the bricks are held tightly in place, and will resist compressive stresses. Each ring must be completed before starting the next.

Vaulted domes (as opposed to corbelled forms) are as easily built and will provide broader curve design potential. In this form, the bricks are laid to provide a smooth concave surface on the interior (Fig. 10.16). Construction must proceed evenly around the perimeter of the dome, closing each masonry ring, or structural failure may result during construction.

**Domes**

FIGURE 10.15. **Corbelled dome. McHenry house, Corrales, New Mexico, 1976. This 6-ft diameter dome was built with semi-skilled labor in a very short time.**

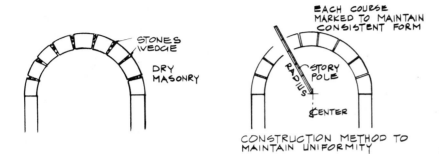

FIGURE 10.16. **Vaulted domes.**

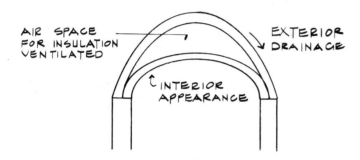

FIGURE 10.17. **Double domes.**

Double domes are common in the Middle East. Their purpose serves two functions. One is the creation of an airspace that will provide additional insulation value. The second is that the exterior shape of the dome may be different, to provide better drainage, than the most desirable appearance on the interior (Fig. 10.17). Ventilation of the air space between double domes is desirable in summer to aid cooling and insulation.

The masonry patterns generated by a combination of vaulting and corbelling can be exposed, or additionally treated for architectural decoration. Decorative treatment of this kind is known as a "stalactite" pattern in Iran (Fig. 10.18). The exterior surface can also be treated with water-resistant fired masonry or glazed ceramic tile for decoration and weatherproofing.

Ventilation and light can be provided either by a hole at the top of single domes in simple structures, or by the use of "lantern" vaults in more complex architectural styles. Lantern vaults are circular or octagonal walls placed on top of a dome, pierced by arched openings, and capped with another dome. This furnishes light and ventilation, providing weather protection as well (Fig. 10.19).

Half domes, or "Ivans," are frequently used for porches, providing both shade and weather protection. They are constructed in a combination of vaulted and corbelled patterns (Fig. 10.20).

**Pyramid Vaults**     Pyramid vaults may also be used to roof square or rectangular room forms. The longer side must be limited in size or the failure stress point will be reached (Fig. 10.21). The shorter ends may also be curved to add strength and reduce stresses of the longer sides, creating an oval pattern.

FIGURE 10.18. **Chehel-Sutun palace, Isfahan, Iran, 1972.** The domed ceiling of this room is finished with a stalactite pattern, which has further been decorated with colored plaster. The origin of this form may have come from the masonry pattern underneath.

FIGURE 10.19. **Mosque, central Iran, 1972. A lantern vault** can be seen in the background, which is a series of arches superimposed on a lower dome, for light and ventilation. The arches are then capped with another dome. Domes are often decorated (and waterproofed) with ceramic mosaic tile, fired brick or cement.

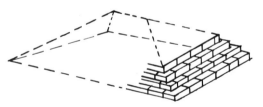

FIGURE 10.21. **Pyramid vaults.**

FIGURE 10.20. **Mosque entry, Kerman, Iran, 1972.** This half dome or "Ivan" serves to protect the entry, like a covered porch. It is also common in residential design. This monumental example also shows the "stalactite" form. The entire structure is sheathed with ceramic tile.

[151]

FIGURE 10.22. **Village street intersection, Faraj, Iran, 1972. This "sail' vault covers four arches.**

**Sail Vaults**        Sail vaults may also be employed, often over four-arched openings in the form of a square. Pendentives are used at the corners, making spring line of the vault vary in height, from the highest point at the top of the arch, to a low point at the pendentive at the corners (Fig. 10.22).

The preparation of working drawings for most vault forms is difficult due to the compound curves and complicated patterns and is generally done by the use of reflected ceiling plans and cross sections at different points. Intersecting points of supporting arches, ribs, and other features can be located on the ground and projected to the vault location by the use of a plumb bob.

**SUMMARY**   1. Roof and floor structures must be adequately designed for anticipated dead and live loads. Upper story masonry walls are best located directly over lower masonry walls.

2. Roof and floor structures should be securely anchored to bond beams or plates, and provided with adequate weight to resist uplift wind forces.

3. Wooden structural members may be embedded in earth walls (i.e. surrounded by earth masonry) above ground level, as long as ground moisture and insect routes are interrupted by a minimum distance of 6 in. (15 cm) of solid earth materials.

4. Mortar joints for vaulted structures of mud brick should be held to a minimum size or wedged with stones or waterproof material.

5. The stresses of vaulted structures should be calculated and analysed.

## chapter eleven

# Insulation and Thermal Mass Values

The insulation value of earth walls has been a subject of heated debate since the inception of modern technology and the establishment of scientific measurement standards. In earlier times, humans had only the ability to know what felt comfortable or what did not, and what modifications made it feel better. Earth buildings are considered on a worldwide scale to be comfortable. Tests conducted by the U.S. Army during World War II determined that the human body was capable of withstanding a much wider range of temperatures and environmental conditions than was previously supposed possible. Mere measurement of temperature and humidity is not enough to define comfort.

The human thermostat with its controls for perspiration and adaption to an existing condition by the use of appropriate clothing and natural physiology enable us to survive in a wide temperature range. It has been only in relatively recent times that interrelationships of temperature, humidity, air movement, and other environmental factors have begun to be understood. This understanding has resulted in the establishment of a new concept termed a "comfort" factor. Comfort is more a comparative value than an absolute one, tempered by what we have experienced and what we have come to expect in the undefined comfort factor.

Ground temperatures measured 3–5 ft (1–1.5 m) below the surface will range from 50–55°F for a large part of the world. This is obviously less than ideal for either winter or summer comfort. By comparison, however, it is a great deal warmer than many winter temperatures, so the ground temperature may be utilized in some mechanical systems. As we vary from the most desirable range, the energy expense for raising or lowering this range is one of degree, in terms of what we can afford economically and what we will accept as tolerable limits. If our tolerable limits can be adjusted, and the limits are lowered (for heating) and raised (for cooling), the task of tempering the environment becomes easier. In the West, we have come to accept the ideal environment as 72°F., although studies indicate that the comfort standard may alter this substantially by the modification of humidity and air movement.

Many areas of the world have different comfort standards, which are tolerable to the people who live there. Tolerable limits will undoubtedly change as the world energy crisis becomes more critical and costly.

People who have lived in earth houses have stated a satisfactory comfort standard repeatedly, more comfortable than temperature measurements might lead us to believe. This gives rise to the traditional belief that adobe houses are warm in the winter and cool in the summer without heating or air conditioning. This may not be precisely true. Earth buildings that have become cold in the winter can be extremely uncomfortable. The same is true for heat in the summer. What earth walls do, however, is to make use of the thermal mass to balance the extremes of the ambient outdoor air temperatures. The indoor temperature will achieve an approximate average between the highs and lows of the outdoor temperatures. The precise balance can be affected by other factors. Sun warmth will accumulate and be stored in the walls during sunny days, even though temperatures may be relatively low. Exterior surface temperatures of earth walls are often higher than ambient air temperatures when in direct sunlight. Wind may reduce this effect somewhat in the form of wind-chill factors. Long periods without direct sunlight will also cause a noticeable cooling effect. Therefore, the warm or cool feel of an earth house may be partly due to thermal mass effect and partly to shading and protection from wind by natural barriers such as ridges, trees, and microclimate wind patterns. If we can enhance and design for such a microclimate, earth material will be even more effective.

## "U" VALUES FOR EARTH WALLS

The insulation values established for earth walls by the American Society of Heating and Air Conditioning Engineers (ASHRAE 90-75) are determined under laboratory conditions in a pure form, that is, without accounting for other environmental factors. The "steady state" U values determined by ASHRAE tests for two typical adobe wall patterns are as follows:*

10 in. (25 cm) thick adobe wall with $\frac{3}{4}$ in. stucco on the exterior, $\frac{1}{2}$ in. gypsum plaster on the interior = 0.263 Btu/ft²/hr/°F.

14 in. (35 cm) thick adobe wall with $\frac{3}{4}$ in. stucco on the exterior, $\frac{1}{2}$ in. gypsum plaster on the interior = 0.203 Btu/ft²/hr/°F.

The apparent poor insulation performance of those earth walls as indicated by those figures can be misleading. Adobe is a traditional, successfully proven material with a good comfort factor, so some element of measurement

* Data source: New Mexico Energy Institute, University of New Mexico, Albuquerque, New Mexico.

must not have been recognized in that test standard. Actual energy use also tends to be somewhat lower than calculations using steady state values, predict.

For this, and other reasons, studies were undertaken to determine thermal characteristics of earth walls, taking into account several additional factors. Brick manufacturers have long held that an "M" (for mass) factor was an important influence in a building's thermal behavior, but no definitive studies had been done. In fact, it appears that heat loss does occur in accordance with U values, but that the thermal mass creates a lag factor, delaying the loss.

A study titled "Transient Thermal Response of Adobe"[1] was undertaken by Dr. Francis Wessling, at the University of New Mexico in 1975. In a computerized model, a 24 in. (61 cm) thick wall was subjected to external wall temperature variations ranging from 15°F to 68°F over 24-hour periods continually for a number of days until a steady state of equilibrium was achieved. A 3 in. (7.5 cm) thickness of fiberglass insulation was placed on the interior to isolate the wall from interior temperatures, which were maintained at 70°F. The article stated:

> The temperatures varied greatly at the outside surface, but only slightly at a position halfway through the wall. The outside variation was 53 degrees and the variation at 12″ (center of the wall) was less than 3 degrees in a 24 hour period. At the adobe–insulation interface, the variation was only a fraction of a degree in the same period. The 24″ adobe wall took approximately 2 weeks to reach a new steady state condition at the interface after the outside temperature variation started. A 12″ wall responded to these same conditions in three to four days. The majority of the attenuation occurred in the first 12″ of the wall.

Wessling further quotes a study done at the National Bureau of Standards in July 1973 by Peary, Powell, and Burch, "Dynamic Thermal Performance of an Experimental Masonry Building,"[2] which yielded similar results. This would lead us to the conclusion that optimum wall thickness for thermal mass effect would be 12–14 in. (30–36 cm).

In response to this need to examine other factors influencing thermal behavior of earth walls, the New Mexico Department of Energy and Minerals authorized a study to determine effective U values.

## EFFECTIVE U VALUES

"Effective U Values—A New Method For Predicting Average Energy Consumption For Heating Buildings,"[3] a study done by van der Meer and Bickle at the University of New Mexico in May 1978, recognized the insulation effect on walls of different compass orientation, local climate facors, and the heat absorption effect of the color of the wall surface. Using typical Meteorological-year climate tapes, the State of New Mexico was divided into eleven climate zones, primarily based on degree days and average losses rather than peak losses. Interpolation was used for areas not covered by specific weather data. A computer model was designed starting with steady state U values, adding factors for local climate, wall compass orientation, and surface-color heat-absorption effects. This resulted in "Effective U Value" charts for 26 types of wall sections, and 2 glazing sections. These types included several adobe brick structures, insulated frame stucco, concrete block, and log designs. The resulting effective U values were far different from the original steady state factors used earlier.

A later revision of this original study was done at the University of New Mexico by Robertson titled "Expanded Revision of Effective U Values,"[4] in February 1981. In this revision, computer codes were improved, weather data was simplified and reduced to four climate zones, and an average period of 7 months (as compared to 6 typical days in the original study) was applied. In a simplifed form, the climate regions are defined by heating degree days (HDD) and cooling degree days (CDD), from a base value of 65°F (see yearly summary). As other factors were used in the calculations, further details can be obtained from the New Mexico Energy Institute, University of New Mexico, Albuquerque, New Mexico.

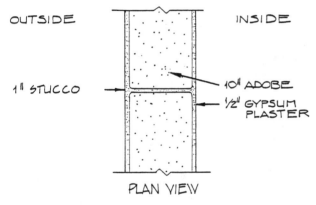

| WALL TYPE 1 | ASHRAE STEADY STATE U-VALUE .240 | | | BTU HR·SF·°F |
|---|---|---|---|---|
| **HEATING EFFECTIVE U-VALUE** | | | | |
| WALL ORIENT· | WALL COLOR | CLIMATIC REGION | | |
| | | 1. | 2. | 3. | 4. |
| EAST | LIGHT | .226 | .217 | .222 | .211 |
| | MEDIUM | .194 | .176 | .178 | .158 |
| | DARK | .161 | .135 | .133 | .106 |
| SOUTH | LIGHT | .218 | .208 | .206 | .197 |
| | MEDIUM | .174 | .152 | .136 | .123 |
| | DARK | .131 | .096 | .067 | .050 |
| WEST | LIGHT | .232 | .224 | .229 | .218 |
| | MEDIUM | .208 | .193 | .194 | .178 |
| | DARK | .185 | .162 | .160 | .137 |
| NORTH | LIGHT | .238 | .234 | .241 | .231 |
| | MEDIUM | .223 | .217 | .224 | .210 |
| | DARK | .208 | .201 | .207 | .188 |

FIGURE 11.1. **Effective U value, 10-in. earth wall.**

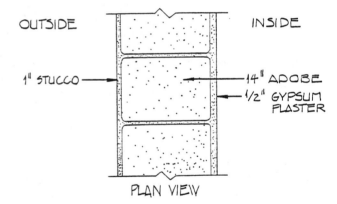

| WALL TYPE 2 | ASHRAE STEADY STATE U-VALUE .189 | | | BTU HR·SF·°F |
|---|---|---|---|---|
| **HEATING EFFECTIVE U-VALUE** | | | | |
| WALL ORIENT· | WALL COLOR | CLIMATIC REGION | | |
| | | 1. | 2. | 3. | 4. |
| EAST | LIGHT | .181 | .174 | .178 | .168 |
| | MEDIUM | .155 | .141 | .142 | .126 |
| | DARK | .129 | .108 | .106 | .084 |
| SOUTH | LIGHT | .175 | .166 | .165 | .157 |
| | MEDIUM | .140 | .122 | .109 | .098 |
| | DARK | .105 | .077 | .053 | .040 |
| WEST | LIGHT | .186 | .179 | .183 | .174 |
| | MEDIUM | .167 | .155 | .155 | .142 |
| | DARK | .148 | .130 | .128 | .109 |
| NORTH | LIGHT | .191 | .187 | .193 | .185 |
| | MEDIUM | .179 | .174 | .179 | .167 |
| | DARK | .167 | .161 | .165 | .150 |

FIGURE 11.2. **Effective U value, 14-in. earth wall.**

|  | Yearly Summary | |
| --- | --- | --- |
|  | HDD | CDD |
| Region 1 | 9058 | 604 |
| Region 2 | 6347 | 960 |
| Region 3 | 4781 | 1388 |
| Region 4 | 3850 | 1762 |

Also included for evaluation were common passive-solar wall components. Effective U values are presented for three typical adobe wall configurations from the revised study below (Figs. 11.1, 11.2, 11.3).

Effective U-values are a good index of average envelope thermal performance . . . (losses) are generally considerably smaller than steady-state U-values . . . Any building envelope component is a passive solar heating device whose performance is a function of absorbed solar radiation . . . color . . . Less insulation is needed than steady-state U-values indicate—perfect for substitution for steady-state U-values into ASHRAE 90-75 . . . far more accurate measure of performance."

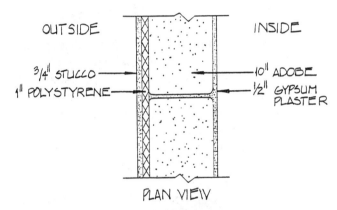

PLAN VIEW

| WALL TYPE 3 | ASHRAE STEADY STATE U-VALUE .107 | | | | BTU HR·SF·°F |
| --- | --- | --- | --- | --- | --- |
| HEATING EFFECTIVE U-VALUE | | | | | |
| WALL ORIENT· | WALL COLOR | CLIMATIC REGION | | | |
|  |  | 1. | 2. | 3. | 4. |
| EAST | LIGHT | .107 | .102 | .104 | .098 |
|  | MEDIUM | .092 | .084 | .085 | .076 |
|  | DARK | .078 | .066 | .065 | .054 |
| SOUTH | LIGHT | .103 | .097 | .097 | .092 |
|  | MEDIUM | .084 | .074 | .067 | .061 |
|  | DARK | .065 | .050 | .037 | .030 |
| WEST | LIGHT | .109 | .104 | .107 | .102 |
|  | MEDIUM | .099 | .091 | .092 | .084 |
|  | DARK | .089 | .078 | .077 | .067 |
| NORTH | LIGHT | .112 | .109 | .112 | .107 |
|  | MEDIUM | .105 | .102 | .105 | .098 |
|  | DARK | .099 | .094 | .097 | .089 |

Courtesy of New Mexico Energy Institute, University of New Mexico, Albuquerque, New Mexico. *Effective U Value—A New Method for Predicting Average Energy Consumption for Heating Buildings*, by David K. Robertson. NMEI Report 76-161C May 1978. (Expanded Revision EMB 2-68-1111 Nov. 1981).

FIGURE 11.3. **Effective U value, 10-in. earth wall with 1-in. polystyrene insulation.**

South-facing windows appear to offer a net heat gain over a 24-hour period, rather than a loss.

An increasing number of governmental regulatory agencies are adopting energy codes, establishing specific performance minimums for the thermal resistance of any given building. The State of New Mexico adopted such an energy code in 1977. As it would be impractical to establish standards for any given building component (i.e. walls, roof, floor, etc.) due to varying architectural considerations, minimum "envelope" values were established. These allowed, for example, larger glass areas, if additional insulation values were incorporated elsewhere in order to provide a minimum overall heat loss. The State of New Mexico has accepted these new "effective U values" for application of the energy code requirements. In most cases, additional insulation is desirable for some earth walls, even with the modified values.

**THERMAL MASS STUDY**   The precise effect of thermal mass in earth walls is now being investigated under the direction of the New Mexico Energy Institute, University of New Mexico.[5] Funding for the research came from several sources, DOE, HUD, and others, and is being overseen by a number of interested groups, including the U.S. National Bureau of Standards.

A field demonstration was needed to evaluate the thermal conductance and thermal-mass effect of earth walls. This study is ongoing at Tesuque Pueblo, New Mexico, with a series of eight test cells of identical size and orientation, carefully constructed of several variations of adobe brick construction, and other cells built of conventional material so that a comparison might be made. Each test cell was built without doors or windows, with foundations and ceilings insulated so that extraneous effects of other features would not influence the measurements. Each test cell is being monitored for wall temperatures at several locations within each wall, for walls oriented north, south, east, and west. Ongoing tests will measure the energy required to maintain constant temperatures, reducing cross-wall radiation effects with baffles and other devices to obtain precise measurements of the thermal performance. Outdoor monitors measure ambient temperatures, wind, sunlight, and climate factors that might have some influence on the test cells.

Unfortunately, results of the study were not available at this writing. Evaluation of the preliminary data indicates that the thermal-mass effect may not be too significant, in terms of insulation value, except during the swing periods where diurnal temperature fluctuations are high. The thermal mass of the walls takes on, stores, and gives off heat, creating a lag between indoor and outdoor temperatures. Preliminary measurements indicate that the indoor-surface wall temperatures tend to be an average of outdoor temperatures in any 24-hour period, with only minor daily fluctuations after stabilization is reached. The fluctuation inside the building will be influenced by the wall thickness (thermal mass) and tends to reach optimum stability at about 12 in. (30 cm) thickness. Thicker walls tend to stabilize longer periods (more than 24 hrs) of seasonal temperature variations. Temperature averages on the inner surface of the wall are only slightly higher than the true average in summer, and slightly lower in the winter. Total effect for a year's performance may offer an advantage of only 4–5%.

The basic heat transfer characteristics of the wall components will ultimately govern the heat loss. The addition of doors and windows, not included for study in this phase of the project, can undoubtedly enhance and make use of the lag effect for both heating and cooling, although the cooling cycle may be more significant, particularly in swing periods of high daily temperature fluctuations. The lag effect may also be useful in areas where energy costs differ between peak-demand and low-demand periods. Heating or cooling energy can be purchased and applied at lower rates, and the effect used when needed, for lower resultant energy costs.

Passive and active solar designs may also make good use of this storage capacity. Fenestration to the south for both walls and clearstory locations can and will accumulate heat in the interior of the building during sunny days. Heat will be stored in the thermal mass and later released by the lag effect.

Further information of the Thermal Mass Study may be obtained when it becomes available from the New Mexico Energy Institute, University of New Mexico, Albuquerque, New Mexico.

One simple answer for increasing the insulation value for earth walls lies in the use of double walls with an air space, or other types of insulation, within the cavity. This configuration was especially common in the construction of farm storage buildings for potatoes and sugar beets in southern Colorado. Winter temperatures in this location can be severe, with lows reaching −40°F (Fig. 11.4). The practice was obviously successful, as many of these above-ground root cellars are still in use.

## DOUBLE WALL CONSTRUCTION

FIGURE 11.4. **Farm storage building, Manassa, Colorado, 1981 (ca. 1930s). This farm storage building for potatoes and sugar beets is built of two 6-in. adobe walls, separated by a 4-in. air space. A portion of the exterior wall has collapsed from lack of maintenance. This is a common type of construction in this part of Colorado which experiences very low temperature.**

The practice of filling the void in double wall construction with additional insulating material has been carried out with little record of the thermal performance. This was not included in either the Effective U Value determination, or the Tesuque Thermal Mass Study. Another solar-energy test project, where pumice was used as an insulating fill, resulted in unexpected problems. Four simple passive-solar test houses were built at the Ghost Ranch (a conference center of the Presbyterian Church) in Abiquiu, New Mexico, and were insulated in this manner. Melting drifted snow on the north side of two structures apparently infiltrated the insulating pumice through cement stucco, or ground moisture entered by capillary action, and ultimately migrated into the exterior adobe wall causing structural collapse without warning. The interior wall remained intact. The insulating fill material went all the way down to the concrete footing, and that may have attracted ground moisture (Fig. 11.5). The cement stucco on the exterior may have also inhibited moisture escape, and the double wall was insecurely bonded together with stretchable poultry netting instead of a more rigid material.

This leads to the conclusion that water-impervious insulation materials should be used in such designs, at least to a point well above ground-moisture sources. The double wall should also be securely cross-tied at regular intervals with header courses of masonry or by mechanical ties.

**APPLIED INSULATION**

It is obvious from the charts presented earlier, that in many instances additional insulation for earth walls is desirable. Without exception, the insulating material is best applied on the exterior of earth walls, unless of course the double-wall system is used. By so doing, the heat transmission through the wall is reduced, and the thermal-mass storage properties are retained for their beneficial effects. An evaluation of each wall orientation and its resultant

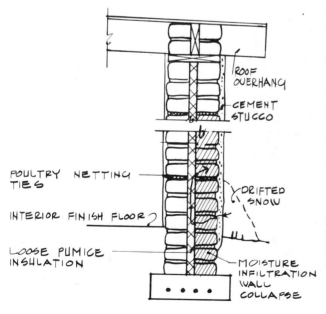

POULTRY NETTING TIES

INTERIOR FINISH FLOOR

LOOSE PUMICE INSULATION

ROOF OVERHANG

CEMENT STUCCO

DRIFTED SNOW

MOISTURE INFILTRATION WALL COLLAPSE

FIGURE 11.5. **Insulated double walls.**

effective U values will help determine the quantity and cost effectiveness of whatever insulation is selected. Several forms of insulation may be used.

Rigid board insulation of the thickness required to create a given heat-transmission factor may be applied to the exterior wall. It should be impervious to water. The major problem with application of this type of insulation is one of physical attachment of the insulating material to the earth wall. It can be attached by nailing it directly to the earth wall. As many insulations of this type are low in tensile strength, it may be necessary to additionally secure the fasteners with tin roofing caps to prevent the fasteners from pulling through the insulation. Nails should be driven at an angle and penetrate the earth wall a minimum of $1\frac{1}{2}$ in. (4 cm) (Fig. 11.6A).

An alternate method would be to attach wood batten nailing strips to the earth wall with gringo blocks or wood anchors, and then attach the insulating board material to the batten strips (Fig. 11.6B). The application of stucco netting and cement stucco over the insulation will additionally secure it, with stucco netting fasteners being long enough to attach solidly in the earth wall. Cracks may occur in the stucco at joints in the insulating material, and these may require additional treatment.

**Rigid Insulation**

One of the most effective earth wall insulations currently available is sprayed polyurethane foam. The material should be of sufficient density, 2.5 lbs/ft$^3$, so as to be nonabsorptive, have good insulation value, but is more costly than some other types. The higher cost, however, may be offset by higher efficiency and lower cost for attachment, required by rigid insulations. The finished surface of the insulation will be somewhat irregular and will echo the shape of the mud wall surface beneath it. This type of material will degrade from direct ultraviolet rays of sunshine, and therefore must be protected with cement stucco. Stucco netting should be stretched over the insulation, attached securely through the insulation into the earth wall, and treated with a standard three-coat stucco. Hairline cracking of the stucco coat sometimes occurs with this type of application, and additional treatment may be necessary. Polyurethane insulations are also used in roofing applications, with several types of protective film which are not suitable for wall applications.

**Spray Insulation**

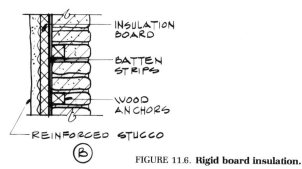

FIGURE 11.6. **Rigid board insulation.**

**EMBODIED ENERGY IN BUILDING MATERIALS**

Walls of earth materials offer big advantages in energy conservation, more in the form of initial energy cost than insulating value. While most energy studies have dealt primarily with efficiency of mechanical heating systems and efficient wall-system components to conserve energy consumption in operating the building, a new focus for the future will be on the energy expended in the manufacture of various building materials. Cement, fired bricks, glass, and steel require large amounts of energy for their manufacture. Further amounts are required to transport raw and finished materials to the manufacturing points, the distribution centers, and the job sites where they are to be used. Earth materials, on the other hand, are generally available close to any building site, and sun or natural climate factors are used to process them.

A comprehensive study of energy costs for building materials was done by the Energy Research Group, University of Illinois, and the architectural firm of Richard G. Stein and Associates, New York, in 1976.[6] Selected items of building material from this study indicate the Btus expended in their production and use:

| | | |
|---|---|---|
| Portland cement | 94 lb sk. | 381,624 Btu |
| Lime, hydrated | 100 lb sk. | 440,619 Btu |
| Common brick ($2\frac{1}{4}$ in. × $3\frac{5}{8}$ in. × $7\frac{5}{8}$ in.) | 1 brick | 13,570 Btu |
| Paving brick ($2\frac{1}{2}$ in. × $3\frac{5}{8}$ in. × $7\frac{5}{8}$ in.) | 1 brick | 24,306 Btu |
| Concrete block (8 in. × 8 in. × 16 in. nom.) | 1 brick | 29,018 Btu |

Although adobe bricks were not included in the above study, the same measurement would yield:

| | | |
|---|---|---|
| Adobe brick (mechanized production) (10 in. × 4 in. × 14 in. nom.) | 1 brick | 2,500 Btu |

A startling fact emerges from interpolating this data into practical terms. *It takes the energy equivalent of one gallon of gasoline to make eight common building bricks.*

The data generated by this study was utilized by the Advisory Council on Historic Preservation in their report "Assessing The Energy Conservation Benefits of Historic Preservation: Methods and Examples."[7] One case study analyzed in the report was the Grand Central Arcade, Seattle, Washington, the adaptive re-use of a hotel in Seattle's Pioneer Square historic district:

> It required one fifth as much energy for rehabilitation materials and construction activities than would have been needed to produce and build a comparable new facility. The rehabilitation "savings" came to more than 90 billion Btu (or over 700,000 gal of gasoline) . . . It annually consumes about 5% more energy than an average equivalent new structure in the same climatic region would if designed in accordance with present day energy conservation standards . . . The Central Arcade will have a net energy investment advantage over an equivalent new structure for the next *two centuries.*

While the embodied energy in existing buildings is not a resource that we can spend, the production of new building materials is an energy expense that needs to be carefully analyzed.

It is obvious that as energy costs increase, the cost of building materials will rise accordingly, making the use of earth building materials more attractive. At some point in the future, it may become necessary to establish an "energy quotient" for various materials, which will determine priorities for building material selection.

**SUMMARY**

1. Wall thickness must be designed for climate, insulation, and cost-effectiveness factors.
2. Social and economic factors may influence design in terms of comfort standards expected or affordable.
3. Selection of heating, ventilating, and air-conditioning equipment should recognize effective U values and the thermal-mass-effect generating lag in the building's requirements.
4. Insulation materials in direct contact with unstabilized earth walls should be of a nonabsorptive type.
5. Careful analysis of wall orientation and final surface color is necessary for maximum performance and cost effectiveness.

**REFERENCES**

1. Francis Wessling, Transient Thermal Response of Adobe, *Adobe News*, #6, Albuquerque, New Mexico, 1975.
2. "Dynamic Thermal Performance of an Experimental Masonry Building," Burch, Peary, Powell. National Bureau of Standards, Washington, D.C., July 1973.
3. L. W. Bickle and W. J. van der Meer, *Effective U-Value—A New Method For Predicting Average Energy Consumption for Heated Buildings*, New Mexico Energy Institute Report #76-161C, University of New Mexico, Albuquerque, New Mexico, May 1978.
4. D. K. Robertson, *Expanded Revision of Effective U-Values*, New Mexico Energy Institute, University of New Mexico, Albuquerque, New Mexico, February 1981.
5. J. Gustinus and D. K. Robertson, Thermal Performance and Energy Conservation Characteristics of Various Sun-Dried Adobe Brick Envelopes, New Mexico Energy Institute, University of New Mexico, Albuquerque, New Mexico. Expected release Spring 1983.
6. *Energy Use For Building Construction*, Energy Research Groups, University of Illinois, Urbana, Illinois, and Richard G. Stein and Associates, Architects, New York, December 1976.
7. *Assessing The Energy Benefits of Historic Preservation: Methods and Examples*, Advisory Council on Historic Preservation, Washington, D.C., January 1979.

## chapter twelve

# Mechanical Considerations

Adobe or rammed earth walls adapt well to most mechanical systems. Earth is a pliable material that cuts easily, patches easily, and can be rearranged as required to adapt to initial installations of piping, ductwork, and electrical systems, and for the later modification of those systems. Most building materials can only be used once and are difficult to cut and shape except in standard patterns. The flexibility and adaptability of earth walls is virtually limitless.

**PLUMBING**

Water, waste, and vent piping can be installed with earth walls either before or after the installation of the walls. Piping can be in place and earth walls laid up to them, or the walls can be built first and simple cuts made in the wall to receive them. The thicker walls in earth construction can usually accommodate most piping. Where large pipes are required, it may be simpler to build a chase using thinner earth walls on each side, the mechanical system occupying the void between them. Most horizontal piping-runs require either difficult cutting in a preplaced wall, which may disturb the structural integrity, or laborious and difficult fitting of the wall to piping systems already in place. The plastic nature of earth walls allows cuts to be made with a hatchet or claw hammer without disturbing the cohesiveness of the wall fabric, as could happen with other masonry materials (Fig. 12.1).

Water and moisture are the primary enemies of earth walls, so pressure testing is suggested prior to final finishing of the wall surface. Plumbing-vent stacks of larger sizes may cause a problem where they must pass through the bond beam. They are best placed prior to construction of the bond beam

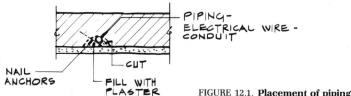

FIGURE 12.1. **Placement of piping and wiring.**

(whether wood or concrete), or may be routed around the bond beam, depending on other wall locations and finishes. Wooden blocks or metal sleeves also may be placed in the form prior to pouring concrete bond beams, so that they can easily be removed to receive anticipated piping that must penetrate the bond beam, without the necessity of cutting the beam after placement.

Wall anchorage for fixtures is best planned and placed prior to installation, but can be installed later, if necessary, in the form of gringo blocks or adobe anchors (chapter seven). In certain locations, alternate wall types may be useful.

Freezing of pipes in an earth wall can cause serious structural damage, although the thermal storage characteristics of earth materials will protect them in most cases. If low temperatures do offer a serious threat, piping subject to freezing should not be placed in north walls, or at least as close to the inner wall surface as possible.

## HEATING SYSTEMS

The heating system chosen for an earth building should be one that takes advantage of, or at least recognizes, the thermal mass and lag effect of earth walls. Passive-solar heating schemes can be very effective, taking advantage of the thermal-storage mass of both exterior and interior walls. The strategic placement of fenestration on the south walls can often reduce heating costs 50% or more at very little increased costs other than a larger window budget. Spaces that are subject to direct solar gain will tend to overheat, so the utilization of such spaces must be carefully considered. The placement of furnishings and selection of finish flooring can enhance or detract from the efficiency of a passive solar system and the liveability of such spaces. Furnishings used in those areas may be subject to damage by sunlight. Care should also be taken with such window arrangements, however, to provide shade, blocking direct sun gain during periods when it is not needed. Superheating of such areas may occur and can often be utilized for heating if air movement or natural ventilation can transfer this surplus heat to another area that does not receive direct solar gain.

## Forced-Air Systems

Forced-air systems may be a logical choice for heating earth buildings. They respond quickly to demands for additional heat, irrespective of the lag factor. They may also be efficiently integrated with economical evaporative-cooling systems, and the air-handling equipment may be utilized to augment and enhance natural air circulation and ventilation, taking advantage of outdoor diurnal temperature variations.

A problem inherent in most forced-air systems is that of zoning different areas that have different heating needs. Living spaces will normally require a higher temperature than sleeping spaces. The zoning problem may be overcome somewhat by the use of more than one furnace or air-handling unit. The cost of two smaller units may be only slightly higher than the costs resulting from one larger unit and large air-handling ducts. Added operational savings will also result from reduced heating costs for lower demand zones.

The arrangement of a direct warm-air heating system is often most effective using a "counterflow"-type furnace. In this system, heated air is pumped downward to a supply plenum, from which it is distributed in underfloor air ducts to floor registers located against outside walls at window locations. The rising warm air, after use, must be collected in a return air system and returned to the top of the furnace for reheating and distribution. Hallways and room spaces may be used for the return air flow to some degree, but the noise level of a large volume of air passing through a small aperture may be excessive.

Such a system will work more effectively if a return air-duct system can be provided, either in an attic space, or in furred down areas of halls and closets. Such a system can also use the return air-collection system as a supply distribution system for evaporative cooled air conditioners. The heated supply ducts in the floor will also provide some radiant heat, warming the floors (Fig. 12.2). Various damper and ductwork combinations may be additionally incorporated to enhance air circulation, taking advantage of outside air temperatures without adding to heating or cooling costs.

**Radiant Heating Systems**

Radiant heating systems are usually either convective baseboard units or of a panel type which is installed in floors, walls, or ceilings. Baseboard-type systems respond more rapidly, and are perhaps better suited for climate zones with high diurnal temperature fluctuations. The panel-type system is slower to respond, and the lag effect of the thermal mass can impair the immediate effect. In climate areas where continuing demand is a factor, or where active-solar systems are in place, radiant panel-type systems are most effective.

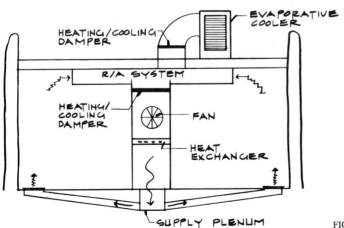

FIGURE 12.2. **Central forced air systems.**

A further problem with radiant systems is their lack of air circulation and ventilation. If an air-cooling system is also required, it will be necessary to provide additional distribution facilities, which can add substantially to the cost. Much of the efficiency of the thermal-mass effect is dependent on air circulation, therefore a radiant system will not be as flexible as a system of the air-handling type. If a floor-panel system is used, it should be placed in a concrete slab for efficient radiation, and insulated against the extraneous effects of natural ground temperatures.

Zoning of radiant systems can be very effective. Electric resistance heaters are readily controlled with individual room thermostats, and hydronic-panel systems use room or zone thermostats acting on valves in the return side of the system.

**Direct Heating Systems**

The use of direct space-heating systems, such as fireplaces, stoves, and space heaters should not be overlooked. The choice of this type of heater will depend primarily on the type of fuel available and the initial costs of installation, which may be higher than other systems.

Fireplaces are the simplest, and a traditional form of space heater. Most traditional fireplace designs are extremely inefficient, but modification, making use of the thermal storage capacity of the earth walls, can raise the efficiency substantially. Combustion air should be supplied close to the firebox in order to reduce the quantity of space-heated air from being drawn out through the fireplace. Normal infiltration from doors and windows may provide adequate combustion air, at least for safety considerations, but a separate outside air source is more desirable and will also allow the rest of the building to be well sealed. Combustion-air damping controls, which will control the draft and lower fuel consumption, should be installed.

The design of the fireplace may also allow for heating of masonry masses in the fireplace structure itself (Rumford design), which gives an additional radiant heat source. The fireplace flue may also be used for this purpose, if constructed in such a manner as to extract and distribute the heat through radiation (Russian design). The flue can be arranged so that most of the heat, which would go outside in conventional design, is transferred to and absorbed by masonry masses.

Unit space heaters, using wood, petroleum, natural-gas fuels, or electrical energy can often augment standard heating systems in areas where intermittent use is required, or where additional means must be used to condition the space with the main system.

**AIR CONDITIONING**

The tempering of air for cooling can be a major consideration in many climates of the world. Often, traditional vernacular practices may offer clues to solving this problem with a minimum of mechanical devices.

Siting and design of the building so as to make use of natural site features, which may inhibit or enhance wind effect, should be considered. It is advisable to examine seasonal demands and effects for both cooling and heating before a final choice is made, because what may be desirable for one season may not be for the other.

Shade for earth buildings, either in the form of deciduous trees or sun-control shading devices built as a part of the structure, can be effective in reducing cooling loads. The thermal mass of earth buildings with adequate ventilation can take fullest advantage of diurnal temperature variations.

Natural cooling systems have been in use for many centuries in the Middle East. Most of them incorporate simple principles making use of lower below-ground temperatures (basements and heat tubes), cooler air temperatures at a distance above ground level (air towers), and water evaporation devices such as fountains. Most of these systems also make use of the natural laws of physics for air movement without mechanical equipment. An in-depth analysis was made by Mehdi N. Bahadori, a professor of mechanical engineering at Pahlavi University, Iran. "Passive Cooling Systems in Iranian Architecture", was published in *Scientific American* (February 1978, pp. 144–154). The several systems examined include air towers, water cistern and fountain effects, as well as the utilization of natural air-circulation patterns. Air-flow diagrams and temperature humidity charts are included.

**Evaporative Cooling**

Evaporative-cooling devices are effective and economical in climate zones that have relatively low humidity. Most incorporate an air-handling fan, and absorptive pads which are supplied with water from a small circulating pump. The pads are kept moist by water-pump circulation, and air is drawn through them with the fans forcing cooled air into the conditioned spaces, creating a positive pressure. Air flow within the building is controlled by the selective opening of vents (windows, doors) that relieves the positive pressure and control the flow. Even in climates with higher humidity, such units will provide some cooling effect. This type of system can be readily integrated with air-handling and heating systems, either in the reverse of the return air flow for heating, or by direct introduction to the supply side (Fig. 12.2). Cooled air may also be pumped directly into the space to be conditioned, but this may be noisier.

**Refrigeration Systems**

Compression–expansion coil refrigeration systems function well, supplying cool, dry air regardless of humidity conditions. The cooling or expansion coil is normally located in the heating system's air-handling unit. The air volume required for cooling may differ from the air volume required for heating, so the sizing of air ducts and equipment may have to be a compromise between what would be optimum for either heating or cooling alone. If the difference is too great, it may be necessary to provide a separate handling system for each cycle. Refrigeration systems are high energy consumers however, and in certain climates cooling energy costs may equal or exceed heating costs.

**ELECTRICAL SYSTEMS**

The installation of electrical systems in earth buildings seldom presents a problem. Regulatory agencies have varying requirements for acceptable standards which may change periodically, so current local building codes should be consulted for compliance.

FIGURE 12.3. **Lathing of wall cuts for wiring. Some building codes require lathing of grooves cut in earth walls for mechanical systems.**

**Concealed Wiring**

Wiring may be installed in earth walls in several ways. Some code requirements allow the use of insulated cable without metal conduit. The wall can be channeled for vertical or horizontal wiring runs (Fig. 12.1). Building-code specifications often require cable of the UF (underground feeder for direct burial) type, when used without conduit. The wiring may also be run in the center of the wall, put in place as the bricks are initially laid. Costs of material and labor for this application may be higher.

The cable or conduit can easily be anchored in the channel cut for it with nails driven into the earth wall. The channel cut is then filled with mud plaster, or with other plaster during the regular plastering schedule. An objection voiced by some code authorities is the possibility of damage to the electrical lines from nails driven into the wall surface for pictures or other purposes, although, if the line is placed deep enough in the wall, this should be of minimal concern. The installation of metal conduit for wiring runs will alleviate the potential problem. Some building codes may also require metal to reinforce the surface that has been channeled (Fig. 12.3), although field experience indicates that this is not necessary.

Electric utility boxes for switches and receptables can be anchored by toe nailing directly into the wall and further secured with mud or regular plaster at the edges. Main electrical service panels may require additional securement in the form of gringo blocks or anchors (Chapter 7).

**SUMMARY**

1. The choice of heating and cooling systems must consider and take advantage of natural environmental and climate factors, available fuels, and resultant operating-cost projections.

2. The insulation values, thermal storage capacity and "flywheel" effect of the lag factor are vital design considerations, and must be recognized and utilized wherever possible. Ventilation is of primary importance.

3. Electrical systems may follow a standard configuration, with special attention given only to the placement of electrical runs and securement of junction boxes in the earth wall.

## chapter thirteen
# Structural Engineering for Earth Buildings

*Gerald W. May, Ph.D.*

DEAN, COLLEGE OF ENGINEERING
UNIVERSITY OF NEW MEXICO
ALBUQUERQUE, NEW MEXICO

Adobe brick and earth wall construction practices have evolved over a period of many centuries in almost all parts of the world. These vernacular construction practices reflected the materials, culture, climatic conditions, and skills available in the particular society. In some cases, such as in the United States, much of the vernacular technology of earth construction has been lost in the last century and must be rediscovered.

As with much building technology that is still in use today, the traditional practices have evolved through trial and error, rather than by the modern sequence of hypothesis, test, implementation. However, earthen buildings can be, and in many cases, must be engineered to satisfy local building code requirements. While some communities do not permit adobe construction, others, especially in the American Southwest, have adopted building codes that embody such principles of practice. In general, structural engineering considerations for adobe construction are similar to those that govern unreinforced (or reinforced) masonry design. In any case, due recognition must be given to the fact that the material and workmanship are more variable than conventional. For this reason, maximum safety factors and conservative structural design are generally desirable in adobe construction. It must also be recognized that many successful earth buildings that have survived for centuries would be in violation of many current building codes. This leads to the conclusion that strict adherance to code standards must be tempered by successful examples from the past.

**MATERIAL PROPERTIES OF ADOBE**

Adobe masonry has many of the same properties as brick masonry, but with one major difference. As the bricks and mortar in adobe walls consist of the same material, the walls tend to be more homogeneous. Thus, the failure cracks in a wall often follow the maximum principal tensile-stress trajectories across the bricks, rather than following the stair-step patterns common in burned-brick and cement-mortar masonry. This property also results in substantial energy loading capacity, or resilience, as evidenced by the difficulty often encountered when an old adobe wall is razed with a wrecker's ball.

In order to be able to use an engineering analysis for a material, its basic properties must be known. In the case of adobe and rammed earth, the important parameters are strength and durability. Over a period of time, some basic tests that are used to insure the basic quality of adobe bricks have come into common practice in the southwestern United States. In some communities, these have been incorporated into the formal building codes. Two of them assess the basic mechanical strength: the compression and modulus of rupture tests, and a moisture-absorption test is specified when water resistance is important.

**Purpose.** To establish the crushing strength of adobe brick.

*Compression Test*

**Procedure.** A statistically valid random sample of the lot should be chosen, approximately 5 out of 25,000. The brick is tested in a flat position, subjected to a uniform compressive load that is gradually increased at a rate of 500 psi/min until failure occurs. The bearing surfaces of the brick must be carefully smoothed or capped with plaster of paris or capping compound so that the stress is uniformly distributed. If plaster of paris is used, it is common practice to first coat the brick surfaces with paraffin in order to prevent moisture migration from the plaster into the brick, or to dry the capped specimen before testing. A true flat platen should be used in the testing machine, along with a swivel head to accommodate nonparallel bearing surfaces.

**Results.** The crushing load is recorded, as well as the dimensions of the bearing surface. The compressive strength is defined as (Fig. 13.1):

$$\sigma = \frac{P}{bl}$$

**Numerical Values.** Many building codes require a strength of 300 psi, with 20% of the samples allowed to drop to 250 psi. Generally, this value is easily attained by reasonable quality adobe brick. In a survey of 60 New Mexico adobe brick manufacturers in 1980, Smith[1] showed that the average compressive strength of all samples was 383 psi, and the average modulus of rupture was 45 psi.

*Modulus of Rupture Test*

**Purpose.** To determine the tensile strength of adobe brick in bending.

**Procedure.** Five bricks out of every 25,000 should be tested to obtain valid results. Bricks should be flat (unwarped) and fully cured before testing. The brick is placed on 2-in.-diameter rollers (pipe can be used) at each end. Another roller is placed at midspan and the load applied through it (Fig. 13.2).

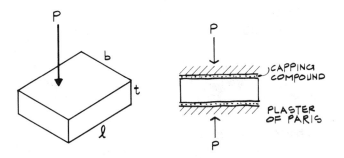

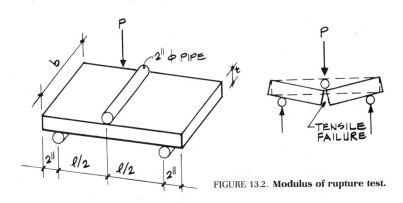

FIGURE 13.1. **Compression test.**

FIGURE 13.2. **Modulus of rupture test.**

Care should be taken to shim the support rollers so that no twisting is introduced during loading. A swivel head should be used on the testing machine for the same reason. The load should be applied at a controlled rate of about 500 lb/minute until rupture occurs.

**Results.** Failure of the brick is in tension of the bottom fiber. The rupture load should be recorded, as well as the dimensions of the support spacing and the brick. The modulus of rupture is the maximum equivalent bending stress in a simply supported beam:

$$\sigma_b = \frac{3Pl}{2bt^2}$$

where $P$ = rupture load (pounds)
    $l$ = span between supports
    $b$ = width of brick
    $t$ = thickness of brick

**Numerical Values.** The modulus of rupture should normally average 50 psi. This value is quite conservative, since bricks should never be subjected to bending stresses in service conditions. An adequate modulus of rupture primarily indicates that the brick can withstand handling stresses without breaking. Smith's investigation showed that semi- or fully-stabilized bricks consistently met this specification.

*Moisture Absorption Test*

**Purpose.** To determine the resistance of asphalt-stabilized brick to the passage of moisture, and hence its durability.

**Procedure.** A dried 4-in. cube cut from a brick is placed on a saturated porous surface for 7 days. It must be carefully weighed before and after the end of the test.

**Results.** The moisture absorbed during the test causes an increase in weight. From the before- and after-test weights, the percentage of moisture increase can be calculated.

**Numerical Values.** The amount of moisture intake should not exceed $2\frac{1}{2}\%$. Bricks that comply with this test are called "treated".

Many building codes specify additional standards for particle-size distribution, allowable shrinkage cracks, and minimum-curing time (see chapter fifteen).

## RAMMED EARTH PROPERTIES

Rammed earth walls are seldom tested after construction in the field, and no definitive strength specifications commonly exist. It has been informally stated by practitioners of rammed earth construction that the strength of damp soil at initial compaction will approximate 30 psi or more, and it will achieve a dry strength of 300 psi or more. They also indicate that even freshly compacted walls are adequate to support normal roof and floor loads, so that construction may proceed prior to full curing. Thicker walls are desirable for rammed earth because they offer more space for easier compaction, and they will be less fragile prior to fully drying. It would be logical to assume, given the same soil composition, that rammed earth is at least as strong as adobe brick. Laboratory tests by Patty in 1939[2] and Clough in 1949[3] confirmed this. Both investigators showed that the compressive strength of rammed earth samples ranged from a low of 462 psi to a high of 850 psi, while brick strengths ranged from 260 psi (by Patty) to 439 psi (by Clough). Patty tested his samples at the end of 6 months of curing, and Clough tested after 2 months. In any event, adequate drying is necessary for higher strengths.

The greater strength of the rammed earth over adobe bricks is due to its greater density when placed. Clough found about a 10% greater dry density in the rammed earth, while Patty observed it less quantitatively.

Since rammed earth walls are constructed with a moisture content of about 10%, it may take many months for them to cure and achieve their full strength.

## DESIGN FOR VERTICAL LOADS

Most of the stresses in a structure will be due to gravity loads. In the case of adobe buildings, the dead loads will generally be substantial, but they are carried by massive walls in which the compressive stresses are not very high.

Gravity loads carried by walls are of various types:

1. Dead loads: There are various dead loads due to the weight of the structure above. These include the weight of the walls, the weight of the tributary area of the roof and any intermediate floors, and any fixed-machinery loads.

2. Live loads: For design purposes, a full snow load on the roof should be assumed. The actual unit load is usually prescribed by the appropriate building code. Any wind on a pitched roof will cause both inward and uplift pressures that are carried into the walls. Occupancy loads must also be accounted for in a multistory building.

Stresses due to these vertical loads must be calculated and added together algebraically. The self-weight (gravity) load in the wall creates a compressive stress of only about 0.7 psi/ft of height, regardless of the thickness of the wall. This value is based on a nominal unit weight of 100 lb/ft$^3$ of adobe. A roof load will, of course, cause a higher stress in a thin wall than a thick one. Stresses are calculated by dividing the load by the cross-sectional area over which it is carried, with no consideration given for the additional section provided by plastering. This assumption only holds true if a number of conditions are met:

1. The bricks must be laid with full slush-mortar joints to insure good load transfer.

2. The wall must be plumb.

3. Any load carried into the wall should be as nearly through the center plane of the wall as possible. Eccentric loads can cause tensile stresses, especially near the top of the wall.

The practical consequences of these criteria are that, even when laid up very carefully, a load-bearing wall should have a minimum thickness. In the United States, a common minimum thickness is 10 in. for a one-story wall and 14 in. for two stories, since these are the basic dimensions of the standard adobe bricks. In addition, since some lack of plumbness and in-plane loading usually occur in the field, maximum height-to-thickness (slenderness) aspect ratios are specified. The numerical values of these ratios depend on the local building codes, with suggested values for earthquake-prone areas as low as 8, and as high as 25 for good quality brick masonry. Table 13.1 shows the maximum wall heights allowed by various practical aspect ratios.

TABLE 13.1
**Maximum Wall Heights (in feet)**

| Wall thickness (in.) | Slenderness aspect ratio | | |
|---|---|---|---|
| | 8 | 10 | 15 |
| 10 | 6.7 | 8.3 | 12.5 |
| 14 | 9.3 | 11.7 | 17.5 |
| 20 | 13.3 | 16.7 | 25.0 |
| 28 | 18.7 | 23.3 | 35.0 |

Higher aspect ratios can be more readily tolerated if the wall is laterally supported at the top, such as by a roof diaphragm, rather than being free-standing. In the latter case, it is conservative practice to design with half of the normal slenderness ratios.

Allowable compressive stresses in adobe must be conservatively estimated. Common practice in masonry design dictates a factor of safety on the crushing strength of at least 5 to 6, giving a reasonable maximum working stress of about 50 psi in adobe. Continuous tensile strength should never be assumed unless there is carefully designed reinforcement of some kind. For instance, in the case of window or door lintels, beams of reinforced concrete or timber should be used to carry the load across the opening, or a compression arch of brick can be used.

**COLUMNS**

Columns, or isolated sections of adobe masonry, should be designed conservatively because the relatively slender section makes them prone to buckling-type failure. If space is critical, timber columns are more efficient in carrying heavy axial loads; however, porticos and porches are often attractively supported with adobe brick columns.

It is common practice, and some codes require it, when using adobe masonry columns, to build with modules of at least 2 bricks. The smallest practical square column then requires four bricks per course. A rational design procedure can be used to predict the allowable loads on a column, as long as the slenderness of the column is accounted for.[4] Table 13.2 shows allowable loads for a typical 10-ft high column of three different elementary cross sections using 10 in. × 14 in. bricks, employing the Uniform Building Code (UBC) procedure:

TABLE 13.2
**Allowable Column Loads**

| Cross-section | Top supported[a] | Top unsupported[a] |
|---|---|---|
| 28″ × 10″ | 12,300 | 9,000 (8-ft max) |
| 20″ × 14″ | 13,100 | 10,000 |
| 24″ × 24″ | 28,000 | 25,800 |

[a] Allowable loads for 10-ft columns.

Such loads as indicated in the table are not often encountered in residential structures, so that factors of safety are usually quite adequate. The main concern is to insure that the column is constructed plumb, and that, if possible, the top of the column be laterally supported by a beam or roof diaphragm. If the loading is not concentric, an eccentricity of up to $\frac{1}{6}$ of the minimum dimension of the column can be tolerated but, at that eccentricity, allowable loads must be derated to $\frac{2}{3}$ of the tabular values.

Lateral loads that enter a structure are generally less predictable than vertical loads, and they often are dynamic, rather than static in nature. The two most common conditions that impose lateral loads are wind and earthquakes.

Wind loads are assumed to act normal to the surface that faces the wind. The intensity of the load can be calculated from the following factors:

1. The maximum probable wind speed for a location
2. The shape of the structure (coefficient of drag)
3. The height of the structure

These are normally combined to give a maximum load intensity for a given location, with a reduction factor to be used if the wall is not flat and rectangular.[4] Generally speaking, unless a masonry building is unusually tall or a wall is freestanding (such as during construction), stresses due to wind loads are not significantly high.

Lateral loads are also imposed on a structure when it is subjected to horizontal accelerations during an earthquake. These are inertial loads which are the mathematical product of the mass and the acceleration magnitude. Mass is high for any kind of masonry, including earth, so that even modest acceleration values can cause substantial inertial loading values.

The actual values of earthquake loading depend on a number of factors, and are not easily calculated exactly without careful mathematical modeling. However, good approximations are in current use. It is not the purpose of this section to discuss in detail the rationale for these equivalent design loads, but rather to point out some qualitative factors that are important. When warranted, an entire analysis should be done according to the applicable design codes.

For design purposes, earthquake loads in a structure are usually modeled as equivalent concentrated loads acting in a horizontal direction. One method for calculating equivalent earthquake loads is given in the UBC. The factors used in modeling the load value in the UBC are:

1. A zone factor, which depends on the maximum predicted probable earthquake intensity for a particular location.
2. An occupancy factor, which assigns a higher factor of safety if the building's collapse would lead to loss of life.
3. A horizontal force factor, which depends on the building configuration and structural type.
4. A factor that depends on the natural frequency of the structure. A flexible system with a low natural frequency will be affected differently than a stiff structure with a high natural frequency.
5. A factor that depends on the site–structure interaction. This basically accounts for differences in soil foundation conditions.
6. The dead load of the structure to be analyzed.

Since there can be no predicting of the direction of earthquake accelerations, these loads are assumed to act in the most critical direction, which is usually perpendicular to the long dimension of the building.

**DESIGN FOR EARTHQUAKE LOADS**

Figure 13.3 shows the idealized action of earthquake loading on a building. A wall will be subjected to in-plane or out-of-plane loading, depending on its orientation to the earthquake acceleration direction.

Observation of failures of low-strength unreinforced masonry in actual earthquakes or controlled tests indicates that there are typical failure modes for both kinds of loads.

In-plane forces cause a wall to rack in shear (Fig. 13.4). The racking load is transmitted into the wall from the roof as well as from the dead load of the wall itself. These loads cause a stress condition of predominantly shear. If the unit shear exceeds the shear strength of the wall, failure occurs. Failure is usually observed as a diagonal crack, since the maximum normal tensile stress occurs at inclined isoclines. Reversal of the acceleration direction causes cracks to open on both diagonals of a wall. The cracking dissipates a great deal of energy and acts as hysteritic damping for the structural response; however, it is serious when these cracks propagate to the corners and a kinematic mechanism is formed. When this happens, the wall usually collapses. There are a number of factors that bear on the occurrence of this type of failure:

1. The thickness of the wall is inversely proportional to the shear stress. A thick wall can more readily carry the racking without serious damage.

2. Any dead load above the wall contributes to the inertial force. A light roof or superstructure is less damaging than a heavy one.

3. Any openings in the wall create stress concentration and reduce the effective section. It is common to see cracks radiating out from corners or doorway or window openings, and damage is usually concentrated in the most slender wall piers. For this reason, openings should be kept to a reasonable minimum, and the slenderness of the piers ($h/a$ ration in Fig. 13.4) kept low.

It is particularly important to keep the slenderness of the corner piers as low as possible, because failure there affects two intersecting walls. When a slender corner pier disintegrates due to shear cracking, partial or total collapse is imminent.

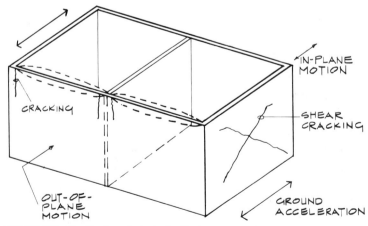

FIGURE 13.3. **Idealized earthquake loadings.**

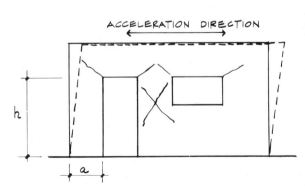

FIGURE 13.4. **In-plane earthquake loading.**

Arya[5] recommends the following conservative rules of thumb for proportioning wall openings in adobe buildings:

1. The slenderness ration ($h/a$) of the outside corner wall pier should be no more than four, and the minimum width should be 4 ft.

2. The total length of openings should not exceed one third of the length of the wall between crosswalls.

3. The bearing length of lintel beams on each side of an opening should not be less than 18 in. (46 cm).

When it is impossible to meet these criteria, the openings should be reinforced with vertical and horizontal reinforcing beams.

Out-of-plane loads cause the walls to flex inward and outward, a phenomenon exactly analogous to intense wind loading. Crosswalls, whether at the ends of the wall or intermediate to its length, act as stiff supports, since they are relatively inflexible in shear. Thus, under high acceleration loads, tension cracks starts at the crosswalls near the top of the wall (Fig. 13.3). These propagate downward and eventually the wall section falls inward or outward. When that happens, the crosswalls lose their bracing and also topple over.

Some of the critical parameters that must be kept in mind for out-of-plane loading are:

1. The unsupported length of the wall should be kept as small as possible. Tensile stresses increase as the square of the unsupported length, so that doubling the length increases stresses by a factor of four. Common practice is to limit the length of an unsupported wall to some value. For instance, the New Mexico Building Code allows a 10 in. wall to span 24 ft without being laterally supported. It is important to note that the critical factor is not the total length of the wall, but the length between crosswalls.

2. The wall must be tied into the crosswalls. If this is not properly done, with interlocking brick courses or reinforcement, the wall loses its support and damage is intensified due to hammering between the disconnected and adjacent walls.

3. A wall that is thickened near the bottom is more seismically resistant than a uniform thin wall. The additional bending section inhibits the collapse of the entire wall even if cracking has occurred near the top.

4. A roof diaphragm is an effective mechanism for bracing the top edge of the wall and transferring the load into the other walls. When the roof is tied into the walls properly, it forms a redundant load path and often prevents the inward or outward collapse of the top of the wall.

Although the typical modes of failure are discussed separately above, it should be clear that they generally occur simultaneously, and that earthquake damage in a building is much more complex than has been described. Other factors that bear on the structure's behavior are its configuration (compactly-shaped floor plans survive much better than unsymmetrical shapes), its foundations, and the surrounding soil conditions.

The most important single factor that every designer of a building must keep in mind is the necessity to tie structural components together. A continuous structure is always more damage resistant due to the redundancy lent by its interconnected parts. Moreover, a redundant structure can often survive partial collapse that would otherwise be catastrophic.

The most critical structural connections are those between adjacent walls, particularly at corners. Many different ways of assuring successful interconnection have historically evolved (Fig. 13.5). The corner buttress is a feature commonly found all over the world in various forms. It is often tapered outward at the base. In its simplest form, it acts as a counterfort that prevents outward tipping of the tops of the wall. In its more refined form, it enhances the interlocking of the corner bricks.

Other details that must be given proper attention with regard to structural continuity are those occurring at door and window lintels, at roof–wall intersections, walls at foundation level, and intermediate crosswall intersections.

The ultimately practical way of assuring that the building does act redundantly is the use of the tie beam (also called ring, bond or collar beam). The tie beam is a ring, or belt, encircling the building near each floor or roof level. It is constructed of a material capable of carrying tension, usually reinforced concrete or heavy timbers, both of which lend themselves to appropriate architectural treatment.

Figure 13.6 shows the typical location of tie beams, either in place of the top course of masonry, or as a continuous lintel beam. The tie beam should

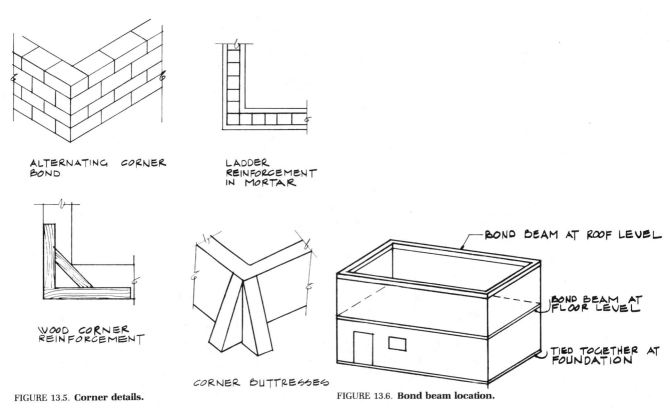

ALTERNATING CORNER BOND

LADDER REINFORCEMENT IN MORTAR

WOOD CORNER REINFORCEMENT

CORNER BUTTRESSES

BOND BEAM AT ROOF LEVEL

BOND BEAM AT FLOOR LEVEL

TIED TOGETHER AT FOUNDATION

FIGURE 13.5. **Corner details.**

FIGURE 13.6. **Bond beam location.**

be continuously reinforced to carry tension, especially at the corners. Typical code requirements specify a minimum size and reinforcement. Clearly, a tie beam should be as wide as the wall is thick in order to assure that frictional forces will be adequate to transfer loads at the beam–masonry interface.

## ROOF STRUCTURES

The design of roof structures for adobe buildings is no different than that for any other type of a building. Common roof structures consist of a plywood or tongue-and-groove deck supported by timber beams. Historically, it was common to use a layer of earth on the deck as insulation; however, modern practice is to use a built-up roofing waterproofing system. Adequate camber and enough drainage scuppers should be provided to prevent the accumulation of rainwater on the roof.

### Domes and Vaults

As mentioned in chapter ten, domes and vaults are also sometimes used to span openings. Although this practice has historically been more common in countries in which timber is in short supply, there is no engineering reason why adobe masonry domes and vaults could not be more widely used.

Shell structures can carry remarkably high loads if they are properly constructed and supported. The stress analysis of many common shapes of shells is well understood, and there are a number of references available for the designer. The following discussion is not meant to be a comprehensive text on shell analysis, but rather to provide some general considerations.

Thin-shell structures derive their strength from the transformation of transverse loads into membrane (in-plane) stresses through arching action, rather than through transverse bending. These stresses can be controlled so that they are only compressive, thus avoiding the necessity of reinforcing the material for tension. It is this basic principle that must be kept in mind for all types of unreinforced masonry shells: loads must only be carried in compression; tension must be avoided. Some other fundamental considerations in shell design include the following:

1. Shells are assumed to be thin if the radius-to-thickness ratio lies roughly between 50 and 1000.
2. Thin-shell theory assumes that the shell is unrestrained against movements due to temperature changes.
3. Loads should always be brought into a shell in a smoothly continuous, distributed manner. Heavy point loads and any geometric discontinuities cause local bending and shear stresses which can cause failure.
4. The state of stress predicted by theory is only achieved when the structure is complete. Stresses during intermediate construction stages should be carefully analyzed, or the shell completely supported during construction.
5. Near the edges of a shell, local bending stresses tend to accumulate. If these stresses are substantial, a shell structure should be gradually thickened near the springing.

Hemispherical and torispherical (partial hemispherical) domes are tractable for analysis, and the regular geometry makes them easy to lay out and construct in the field. They can also be used to cover a square ground plan by providing squinch arches at the corners, as is often the case in Moorish architecture. Figure 13.7 shows the definitions for a hemispherical dome.[6]

The two principal membrane stresses in the shell are the circumferential stresses $\sigma_\theta$ and the meridional stresses $\sigma_\phi$. Shear stresses may be calculated as shown in Fig. 13.8 using transformations from the principal directions. These stresses vary when the shell is subjected to a uniform gravity loading ($q$ in lb/ft$^2$).

The meridional stresses are always compressive, varying from 0.5 $rq/t$ at the top to 1.0 $rq/t$ at the bottom edge. The circumferential stresses, however, vary from compression in the top to tension in the bottom. Under the uniform gravity loading, the transition from compression to tension occurs at a central angle value of 51°49'. Under a uniform snow load, distributed over the projected area of the shell, the transition occurs at 45°. Thus, for most practical loads, a torispherical shell with a total central angle of 90° will have compressive stresses everywhere (Fig. 13.9).

The maximum compressive stress occurs at the edge, in the meridional direction, and is equal to about 0.6 $rq/t$. The circumferential stress approaches zero at this same point. Applying this stress analysis to adobe material indicates that a dome with a span of over 100 ft is feasible.

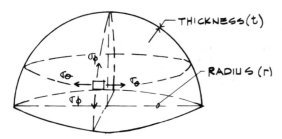

FIGURE 13.7. **Definition sketch for hemispherical shell.**

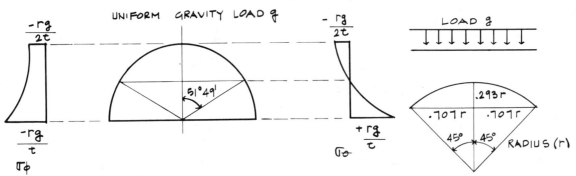

FIGURE 13.8. **Stress distribution in hemispherical shell.**

FIGURE 13.9. **Compressive torispherical shell segment.**

In anything but a complete hemisphere, the support reactions have both vertical and horizontal components. This is a very important structural limitation, since the arching forces can be substantial. The vertical components can be carried through columns or vertical walls, but the outward component must be resisted in some way, such as with inclined walls or buttresses. Another common solution is to construct a reinforced concrete ring beam around the outside edge of the shell (Fig. 13.10). The arching forces act outwardly on the ring beam, causing tensile forces that are carried by reinforcement in the ring. Thus, the shell with the ring becomes an integral, self-equilibrated structure which must only be supported vertically.

A catenary shape is one defined by a chain hung from two supports. Its distinguishing feature is that it most nearly approximates a purely compressive arch shape. The catenary shell is somewhat deeper than the torispherical, but has no other distinct advantage.

Cylindrical shells, or barrel vaults, can also be used, especially if they are used in multiples. Their analysis is analagous to arches. Again, horizontal thrust must be accomodated at the ends.

Construction of shells with adobe or other masonry requires a good deal of ingenuity, since the shells require three-dimensional definition of all points. In the Middle East, construction of small shell structures without

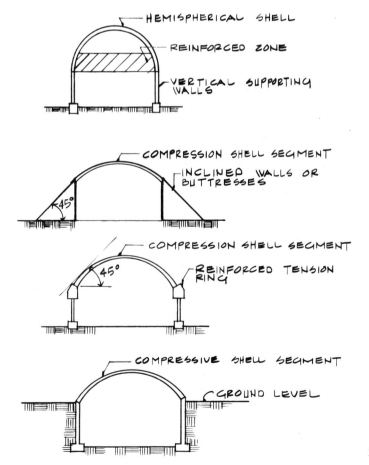

FIGURE 13.10. **Shell support details.**

supporting scaffolding is commonplace. The bricks are usually smaller than the common American sizes, and are laid up in complete circular courses. The shape is maintained by using a rod of fixed length pivoted about the center of the imaginary sphere.

**SUMMARY**

1. Earthen structures can be engineered. With even modest quality control during manufacture, adobe bricks have predictable strength which can be designed into a structure. The key design consideration is to keep all stresses in the structure in a compressive mode, since the tensile strength of adobe masonry is very low. Most indigenous building methods that have developed over the history of humankind have produced workable solutions to this problem. The designer can often learn a good deal by observing what has evolved.

2. It is also very important to emphasize that many areas in which adobe is commonly used are seismically active. The extra cost of designing some earthquake-resistant features into a structure are modest, and certainly necessary to consider. The incorporation of some of these simple concepts would in themselves have prevented many of the catastrophic failures seen in such earthquake areas as Iran, Morocco, Peru, and China.

**REFERENCES**

1. Edward W. Smith, *Adobe Bricks in New Mexico*, Circular 188, New Mexico Bureau of Mines and Mineral Resources, Socorro, 1982.
2. Ralph L. Patty, Puddled-Earth and Rammed-Earth Walls, *Agricultural Engineering*, **20,** No. 8, p. 60–61, August 1939.
3. Richard H. Clough, *A Qualitative Comparison of Rammed Earth and Sun-Dried Adobe Brick*, University of New Mexico Publications in Engineering No. 4, Albuquerque, 1950.
4. *Uniform Building Code*, 1982 Edition, International Conference of Building Officials, Whittier, California, 1982.
5. A. S. Arya, *A Manual of Earthquake Resistant Non-Engineered Construction*, Indian Society of Earthquake Technology, Roorkee, India, 1982.
6. A. M. Haas, *Thin Concrete Shells*, Vol. 1, John Wiley & Sons, New York, 1962.

## *chapter fourteen*
# Repair and Renovation of Earth Buildings

The first step in any repair, renovation, or restoration is the determination of the use to which the completed project will be put, the probable life span of that particular use, and possible future restorations. Most buildings ultimately serve a number of purposes, all of which may not be predicted in advance. Therefore, the basis of sound planning for flexible future use should be considered. These plans may be modfied, but if they are examined first, the design decision will be an educated one and may mitigate future problems and expense.

The budget available for restoration or stabilization will be the governing factor in whatever work is to be undertaken. Only by careful cost estimation can the necessary budget be determined. The cost of preparing an estimate with possible alternatives and realistic probable costs is the initial step in any restoration program. The failure of many restoration programs is the result of a lack of such a determination. Buildings of historical importance can be restored only to preserve the heritage of the resources, even though economic usefulness may not be the major consideration. Most restorations, renovations, or adaptions, however, must be economically viable or the project will ultimately fail. Possibilities of adaptive, economically viable use must be determined and evaluated from careful cost estimating and the life-cycle cost benefits.

Measured drawings must be prepared before any accurate cost estimates can be made. This must include a reasonable determination of the details of foundations, building sections, and structural details. The scope of the investigations and drawings may be staged as well as the physical work of stabilization, renovation, or restoration to conserve cost, and may go hand in hand with cost estimated from the preliminary stage to final details.

Repairs to an existing building may assume several forms:

Stabilization
Renovation
Restoration

**STABILIZATION**     The major enemy of earth buildings is water. Stabilization must include measures to stop further deterioration, and may logically include long-range structural repairs necessary to make the building structurally sound. The first may be temporary measures, such as wall bracing to prevent collapse, and may go on to replace or reposition walls and make permanent repairs correcting the cause of the problem.

Short-term water flows from broken plumbing or roof gutters can cause severe damage to earth buildings in a very short time. Often the more serious threat to the building is the pervasive influence of long-term water damage that erodes and undermines walls, sometimes in areas where it cannot be readily observed until structural failure occurs. Stabilization of an earth building starts with making sure that it is dry. Ambient rainfall itself seldom is the major cause of damage and continuing deterioration. The major long-term factor is drainage and the control of concentrated water flow. The natural moisture found in most soils can be a major factor. Most old earth buildings were originally sited with surface drainage reasonably well established, since the original builders were aware of the water-control problems. The effect of natural soil buildup, possibly in part from erosion of the building wall fabric itself, natural soil buildup, and later man-made site drainage changes can have a serious effect. As a result of any of these factors, floor grades within the structure may ultimately occur below exterior ground levels. Earth walls when dry are strong, with compressive strength adequate to support wall loads. When walls become damp all the way through, from whatever cause, the dead load of the wall above can cause structural failure or serious damage to the fabric of any exposed portion of the below-grade wall that is unsupported (Fig. 14.1A).

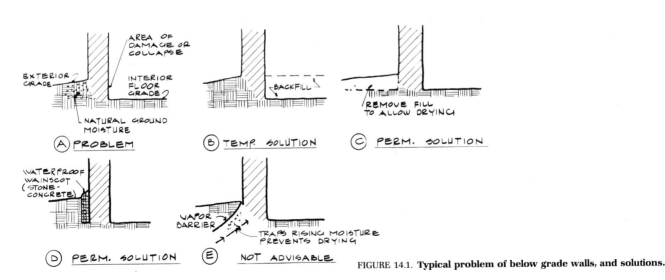

FIGURE 14.1. **Typical problem of below grade walls, and solutions.**

[186]

A temporary solution to prevent collapse may be the simple backfilling of the below-grade portion of the wall, to support and preserve it, until plans and costs of more permanent repairs can be made (Fig. 14.1B).

One permanent solution is to remove the soil buildup and restore the original grades (Fig. 14.1C). This may be impractical for reasons of cost or other site considerations. Another more practical solution may be to build a waterproof barrier, perhaps with structural qualities similar to concrete, particularly if the base of the wall has been damaged, filling in eroded areas and acting as a vapor barrier to allow drying of the exposed below-grade portion of the wall (Fig. 14.1D). Vapor barriers should be used with caution, however, as they may impair natural drying. Inherent ground moisture normally rises to the nearest dry surface, and vapor barriers can trap moisture in a location where it may be even more damaging (Fig. 14.1E).

Another drainage problem is that of periodic severe runoff of collected and concentrated rain water flows from roofs or site drainage. The damage from this type of runoff can be even more critical than basic drainage problems. Concentrated streams of water, from such sources as a frozen water pipe, can seriously damage and destroy structures in a matter of hours, although the damage may be limited to the localized area of water flow. Deep flooding will destroy most earth buildings unless they are protected with some form of waterproof plaster that also acts structurally to support the wall.

The most common form of damage to unprotected earth walls is basal coving. It is a common problem that is found worldwide (Fig. 14.2). This type of damage seems to be caused by rain splash at the base of the wall. Rain water rundown will wet the base of the wall more deeply, and splashing rain at the junction of the wall and the ground causes additional physical erosion at that point. This may be accelerated and aggravated by capillary moisture rise in the wall from ground water. In some instances, this capillary water will contain dissolved salts and minerals, which on drying will recrystalize and fracture the wall fabric. Freeze–thaw cycling may also be a factor, although this seldom seems to be a problem with standing earth walls. Basal wall coving is more a cosmetic flaw in most cases than a serious short-term threat to the wall, unless it progresses to a point where the center of gravity and compressive strengths of the wall are compromised. Wall coving may occur to incredible depths before the wall will collapse, attesting to the compressive strength of the earth wall. The most satisfactory from of repair is to replace the coved area with earth-mortared earth brick or mud plaster, depending on the depth that must be repaired. Loose, spongy material must first be removed, and care must be taken to insure that the new material adheres to the existing wall fabric.

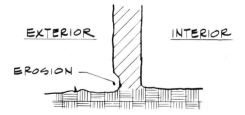

FIGURE 14.2. **Wall base coving.**

**RENOVATION**     The renovation must be as carefully planned as a new building, perhaps even more so. These considerations must include expected use, traffic patterns, and the addition, replacement, or repair of mechanical systems and building features such as doors, windows, and finish details.

A careful determination of what is in place and its condition may determine which portions of the building's features and mechanical systems may be utilized. This information, indicated on the measured drawing, will be utilized when planning changes, or with the redesign of the improvements and revised costs.

Renovation is more concerned with practical answers to the needs of adaptive use than the accurate reproduction of features as they were in the past. Historical accuracy, for the most part, can be ignored, and the primary concern is to make the most practical use of what is in place at the least cost that will result in an acceptable appearance. Removal or destruction of some features of the building may be necessary, acceptable, and expected.

It should be noted that some governmental jurisdictions may provide substantial tax advantages to encourage restoration and adaptive use of older buildings. These should be investigated thoroughly prior to any final decisions on renovation details, as the tax incentives may require approval before construction to qualify. Failure to comply with the regulations may result in the loss of tax benefits.

Building codes may offer additional complications for both renovation and restoration in that, under certain circumstances, the building features may be required to be brought up to current code standards. In most cases, old work is allowed to remain as is unless obviously dangerous to life and safety. The conditions for code upgrading requirements may be contingent on the amount of work to be done, either by percentage or cost limits.

**RESTORATION**     True restoration poses a number of complications in addition to the usual ones for building renovation. As much as possible should be determined of the building's history at the very outset, before any definitive decisions are made. This information may be in the form of original plans in archival locations, to books and newspaper stories and historical photos. Oral history will be of interest, but may not be very accurate. One may need to include the archaeological aspects of excavation and the destruction of building details that will offer clues to the building's history. Few buildings are built precisely as originally planned, and changes during initial construction may have been made. Most buildings are further modified periodically to suit changing tenant needs and owner desires. These changes might logically be expected as often as ten-year intervals. Thus, a building that is 100 years old may have undergone 10 major changes.

An early tentative decision for restoration that must be made is the time period for which the building will be designed and presented. Certain features may be missing and must be substituted with authentic replacements, which may not be possible, or interpreted and created from new materials. We then have the decision to either differentiate between original and new, by color, form, special treatment or texture, or to reproduce the replacements as closely as possible without differentiation. The careful delineation between old and new will be most demanding and the most costly. Depending on the historical importance and the projected use, it may be unnecessary. Most restorations, which will be put to active, current use, may be mainly visual in character. We are able, in this case, to utilize modern materials and techniques to soundly rebuild, as long as the visual appearance is reasonably accurate historically, and compatible with existing features that may be left in place.

Typical details of many old earth buildings are detailed in Figs. 14.3 and 14.4. Features may be found singularly, and in various combinations. Repairs

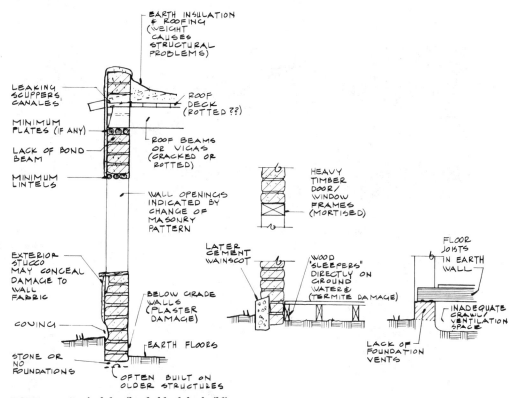

FIGURE 14.3. **Typical details of old adobe buildings.**

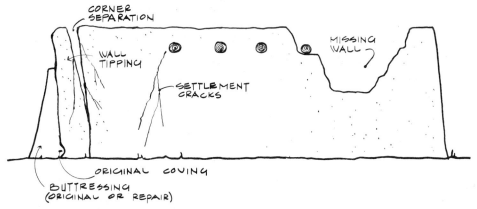

FIGURE 14.4. **Typical elevation of old adobe buildings.**

done over the life of the building may conceal original details and offer clues to the age of the repairs. Many of the repairs may themselves assume historical significance. The renovation of one project is shown in Figs. 14.5 (before) and 14.6 (after).

FIGURE 14.5. **Olson house, Albuquerque, New Mexico, 1976 (ca. 1915).** (*a*) **Before renovation, this house had many problems, including sagging structure, poor foundations, and peeling stucco. Most problems were caused mainly by bad subsoil conditions, neglect and ill advised repairs. Some of the repairs caused more harm than good.** (*b*) **Multiple layers of stucco to patch cracks in sagging walls over a 60-year period were ineffective due to faulty site drainage and foundations.** (*c*) **Expansive clay subsoil, leaky plumbing and poor foundation design caused ongoing problems. Some foundation repairs had caused even further problems, directing rainwater flow into the subsoil at the foundations.**

(a)

(b)

FIGURE 14.6. (*a, b, c*) **Olson house, renovation project complete.**

An outline for the stabilization, renovation or restoration of earth build-ings should include the following:

1. Historical investigation
   (a) Archival resources
   (b) Make measured drawings
2. Determine problems
   (a) Prevent imminent structural failure, emergency measures
   (b) Wall movement, determine causes
   (c) Other structural problems
3. Dry out the structure
   (a) Correct causes of concentrated water flow damage
   (b) Established adequate site and building drainage
4. Determine future utilization possibilities
   (a) Alternative uses
   (b) Viable economic projections
5. Select appropriate details
   (a) Structural finished, cosmetic treatment
   (b) Door and window types, details
   (c) Mechanical considerations for plumbing, heating and electrical work
6. Sequence schedule for priorities
7. Prepare detailed cost estimate for various stages, with contingency allow-ances
8. Funding sources

## chapter fifteen
# Building Codes for Earth Construction

The use of earth as a building material in many geographic areas of the world is an economic necessity. In economically depressed areas, shelter must be constructed with as little outlay of cash as possible. Many of the refinements that more wealthy economies take for granted, or insist on in the form of building codes, are simply not possible. While building codes are designed to insure minimum quality standards, in these areas building codes must logically assume the form of guidelines and instruction rather than one of regulation. If highly restrictive and unrealistic codes are enforced, they may deny the people of one of their most pressing needs.

Certain areas of the world, and particularly the third world countries, are prime examples of this need. Many rural areas, often with severe economic problems, have immediate need for low-cost, economically viable housing and other utility structures. In the normal economic framework, the capital necessary for building is supplied by savings banks and various types of funding institutions and governmental agencies. These institutions are influenced to some degree by the regulatory authorities, therefore the application and enforcement of unrealistic codes can also deny the owner the sorely needed capital with which to build.

**CURRENT BUILDING CODES**

Current building codes in various parts of the United States differ greatly in their requirements for "Unburned Clay Masonry" (adobe). The "Southern Building Code" (Southern Building Code International, Inc., 1976 edition with 1977–78 revisions) makes no mention of this material. The "Uniform Building Code" (1982 edition) (International Conference of Building Officials, Whittier, California) in wide use in the western United States, recognizes the material, but limits its regulation to four paragraphs, which are strongly restrictive (appendix b). The "One and Two Family Dwelling Code" is a code compiled by several authorities for residential construction, and makes no mention of unburned clay masonry, and none deal with rammed earth.

Various state, county, and municipal areas may be governed by the jurisdiction of one of the major codes, but add amendments to or make substitutions for specific provisions in light of local tradition or economic pressures. The state of New Mexico has adopted the most comprehensive earth building code as an amendment to the UBC (appendix a). The New Mexico Amendment has been and is being used by other jurisdictions for amending their codes. However, many of these bodies have modified the New Mexico Amendment, sometimes to reflect the local climate and traditions. It must be noted that building code provisions are constantly being revised and current provisions need be determined for compliance.

Each building code has its own form and order for dealing with various provisions that are of importance, and may not follow the form chosen for presentation here. The areas of specific regulation are broken down into eight main headings, and various provisions within each heading are broken down into subheadings.

1. Structures, adobe and rammed earth
2. Foundations
3. Specification for untreated bricks
4. Specifications for treated bricks
5. Specifications for pressed bricks
6. Mortar
7. Rammed earth walls
8. Plaster and protective coatings

Each of the eight categories are dealt with individually by (1) Commentary on need, and (2) Recommended code requirements. In the determination of the value and need of each provision, it is necessary to recognize the basic limitations imposed by the materials and technology, local environmental considerations, and to strive to determine adequate minimums. The key word is "adequate" as opposed to "best". Many jurisdictions have no codes or do not enforce them, so our purpose here is one of establishing guidelines rather than regulations.

**SUGGESTED CODE MODEL FOR EARTH CONSTRUCTION**

**A. Structures**

1. Building Height

(a) Why should there be an arbitrary limit on the height of earth structures? The Taos Indian Pueblo in New Mexico is five stories high and has been continuously occupied for more than 1000 years. Multistory buildings of earth in other parts of the world are also common, some reaching a height of ten stories or more. Physical properties of the material may limit this in practical considerations, but many codes appear to be arbitrary.

(b) Recommend that height not be limited, if wall height/thickness ratios are adequate for stability in expected wind and seismic loadings, soil bearings, and compressive strength of the wall.

## 2. Wall Thickness

(a) The wall thickness is of relatively little importance as long as height/thickness ratios are considered. Successful walls in the Middle East range from 4 in. (10 cm) to 10 ft (3 m) or more.

(b) Recommend minimum thickness of 4 in. (10 cm) for interior curtain walls, 8 in. (20 cm) for interior nonbearing walls, and 10 in. (25 cm) minimum for bearing walls of single story, and 14 in. (35 cm) for the lower of two-story bearing walls. Note: Thick walls may take a considerable length of time to dry and reach full compressive strength. If multiple brick walls are designed, care should be exercised in the quantities laid at any one time to allow time for drying. Mortar moisture may infiltrate the brick causing structural weakness. A simple field test for dryness is described in Chapter 4. Drying time will vary with initial wetness of the mortar, humidity, and other factors.

**Rule of Thumb:**
Single-brick walls:  7 courses daily maximum
Double-brick walls:  3 courses daily maximum
Triple-brick walls:  2 courses daily maximum

## 3. Wall Height/Thickness Ratio

(a) The compressive strength of earth bricks/walls is usually lower than that of other conventional masonry materials. Table 9.1 calculates actual wall loadings, indicating that it is unlikely that most wall designs could overload the compressive strength of most earth bricks/walls. Unofficial observations indicate that a ratio of 10/1 is common on a worldwide basis for bearing walls. Curtain/partition walls are often less.

(b) Recommend that a minimum of 10/1 ratio be maintained for bearing walls, and that wind and seismic loading for various areas be calculated, without arbitrary limitations.

## 4. Wall Length Without Cross Support

(a) Any wall will be subject to wind and seismic loadings, the severity of which will be reduced by perpendicular cross-wall support. Common code requirements establish a maximum of 24 ft (7.3 m) for single-story walls.

(b) Recommend that wind and seismic loadings be calculated, in conjunction with 2 and 3, above.

## 5. Brick Bonding

(a) Standard masonry practice indicates an ideal bonding of 50% of the length of the brick. Practice in the earth brick industry (worldwide) approximates a standard of 3–5 in. (8–13 cm). As the bricks and mortar are of the same composition, a homogenous structure results.

(b) Recommend a minimum bonding of 4 in. (10 cm).

## 6. Tie Beams

(a) Standard masonry practice requires a bond or tie beam at the top of the wall, or at regular intervals depending on wall height, to stabilize the wall. In the case of earth walls, a double purpose is served: as a plate to distribute concentrated roof-structure loads, and further as a collar to prevent wall movement and separation at the corners. The attachment of the tie beam to the top of the wall is a further matter to be considered. Industry practice does not normally include mechanical fastening of the tie beam to the top of the wall, depending on roof structure and additional wall weight above to resist uplift forces. Additional anchorage into the wall would only lower the stress point. Historic buildings seldom had tie beams, but most used isolated plates to distribute concentrated loads.

(b) Recommend a tie beam of wood or reinforced concrete be placed at the top of earth walls, or at intervals so that the wall height/thickness ratio be maintained. Minimum thickness of 4 in. (10 cm) times the thickness of the wall, or with a bearing of at least 4 in. (10 cm) on any masonry course at the top of the wall. If a wood tie beam is used, it should be suitably mortised to prevent end separation, or if made of multiple small members, overlapped and nailed to prevent lateral separation. If concrete is used it should be reinforced with two deformed rebars of $\frac{3}{8}$-in. (1 cm) diameter. Additional horizontal reinforcement in the form of patented masonry reinforcement at regular intervals may reduce the requirements for tie beam size. Environmental factors may suggest further analysis for wind or seismic forces.

### 7. Attachment of Roof Structures

(a) Roof structures are normally attached to the tie beam. Industry practice includes toe-nailing into wood tie beams, or the placement of metal strap anchors in the concrete beam as it is poured. Power driven fasteners also can be used.

(b) Recommend that positive attachment of roof or floor structures be made with toe-nailing to wood, inserted steel straps in concrete, or power driven fasteners.

### 8. Lintels

(a) Lintel strength requirements are ideally determined by formula, taking into account the type of material, span, bearing on each end, "flat arch" effect of masonry walls above the opening, and concentrated roof loads.

(b) Recommend minimum thickness of 2 in. (5 cm) for spans to 5 ft (52 cm), 4 in. (10 cm) thickness for spans to 9 ft. Make calculations for spans in excess of 9 ft. Lintel bearing on adobe walls to be a minimum of 8–12 in. for each end.

### 9. Attachment of Abutting Partitions

(a) Wood frame and adobe walls abutting earth walls must be secured, principally against shear stress. If both sides of the corner are to be plastered, reinforcing lath corners and minimal attachment is adequate, such as toe-nailing of frame partitions to the earth walls directly, or minimum masonry ties of metal lath with earth walls. If more positive securement is required, earth wall intersections should be laid up solid as the wall is built, chipped out for toothing of bricks or toothing of abutting rammed earth walls to a depth of 4 in. (10 cm). Frame walls can be fastened to wood nailing blocks laid in the wall as built, or with wooden wall anchors (Fig. 7.10).

(b) Recommend minimal attachment for curtain walls, and positive attachment for bearing walls. Positive attachment should consist of wooden wall anchors inserted in the wall, or masonry ties of metal lath (2.5 lb/ft²) a minimum of 6 in. (15 cm) wide by 36 in. (90 cm) long, one half of the length nailed to the first wall vertically, and the other half placed between courses of the abutting wall as it is laid, not more than 24 in. (61 cm) apart.

## 10. Pier and Column Size

(a) The large size of most adobe bricks must generate large piers and columns to provide multiple-brick masonry. Earth walls are strong in large masses (compressive strength) but weak in tensile strength, also generating a requirement for larger columns.

(b) Recommend a minimum column size of 28 in. (71 cm) in one dimension and 20 in. (50 cm) in the other, unless seismic requirements indicate more. Note: Window and door openings shall not be located closer than 28 in. (71 cm) from any corner.

## 11. Parapet Walls

(a) Parapet walls are common in many architectural styles. The additional weight can add significantly to roof-structure anchorage, and establish positive water-flow control.

(b) Recommend that parapet walls be required on all flat-roof construction to a minimum height of 8 in. (20 cm) above the roof surface. Higher parapets may be required for party walls of certain occupancies for fire control.

## 12. Fireplaces

(a) Adobe bricks or earth walls provide a satisfactory material for fireplaces. High temperatures in the firebox may cause firing of the surface, resulting in spalling of the hardened surface.

(b) Recommend that earth walls be allowed for fireplace construction when used in conformance with standard masonry fireplace requirements for firebrick, and seismic reinforcement. When fireplaces are built to an existing wall, suitable toothing or reinforcement, similar to those for attaching abutting walls, should be done.

## B. Foundations

### 1. Basement and Foundation Walls

(a) Unstabilized earth walls should not be used below grade, or for basement walls, as they may absorb ambient moisture and thereby lose structural strength.

(b) Recommend all foundation and below-grade walls be built of waterproof materials.

### 2. Foundation Wall Height

(a) Waterproof foundation walls should be built to a height above finish grade to prevent the rise of capillary moisture which might weaken the earth wall, and to reduce coving erosion.

(b) Recommend foundation wall height extend a minimum of 6 in. (15 cm) above adjacent finish exterior grades. Interior foundation walls shall extend to the height of the finish floor, or to an additional height of 4 in. (10 cm) above concrete slabs for protection during construction.

### 3. Foundation Wall Thickness

(a) Foundation walls should be adequate to support the wall above it. Omission of the space required for perimeter insulation is acceptable if wall loadings are not excessive.

(b) Recommend that foundation walls be as thick as the wall it supports. The thickness of perimeter insulation may be substituted if it does not exceed 20%.

### 4. Footings

(a) Footings need be only strong enough to support the wall weight above, considering allowable soil bearing. If foundation footings are placed on highly expansive clay substrate, they should be designed as grade beams to resist uplifting or subsiding soil pressures. Gravel footings are allowable providing suitable percolation for drainage is provided. Footing depth for solid footings needs to be below expected frost depth to prevent heaving.

(b) Recommend that footings be designed to adequately support wall weight, plus allowances for expansive soils, and placed below frost depth or be of gravel suitably drained.

**C. Specifications For Untreated Bricks**

### 1. Soils

(a) Suitable bricks may be made from a wide variety of soils, with a clay content that can range as low as 5% to a high of 30%, and from aggregates that contain a high percentage of coarse aggregate and rocks. There is more often too much clay rather than too little. Soils and clay types may be analyzed, but making sample bricks from the soil proposed for use is most effective. High clay soils may require tempering with sand or straw to make satisfactory bricks.

(b) Recommend that suitable soils be used so that the bricks will test satisfactorily, tempering the soil as necessary.

### 2. Water for Mixing

(a) Water for mixing is of little importance unless a high quantity of soluble salts are present that could recrystalize upon drying, damaging the bricks.

(b) Recommend that brackish, high salt-content water not be used for mixing.

### 3. Curing Time for Bricks

(a) Curing time for bricks cannot be stated other than to require that bricks be dry before use. Curing time will depend on temperature, humidity, wind, and amount of water used in mixing, and may range from as little as 4 days up to several weeks. If the bricks are not reasonably dry, they cannot be handled.

(b) Recommend that bricks be dry before using.

### 4. Testing of Brick Samples

(a) Random sampling of bricks for testing is a routine matter. A few samples out of each thousand will indicate the quality of the bricks. Laboratory testing can be undertaken to determine clay content, compressive strength, modulus of rupture, and moisture content. Clay type may also be determined by X-ray diffraction. Simple field tests may be undertaken that will approximate the laboratory tests (chapters four and thirteen).

(b) Recommend random testing be done at the ratio of 5/5,000 or at the discretion of the building official, as follows:

Clay Content: 15–25% by particle size (laboratory), or by appearance in field. Bricks should have minimal cracking, with a maximum of three cracks $\frac{1}{8}$ inch × 3 inch (3 mm × 8 cm). Excessive cracking indicates too much clay, too little may indicate not enough.

Compressive Strength:   Minimum 200–300 psi (laboratory).
Modulus of Rupture:   Minimum 40–50 psi (laboratory).
Moisture Content:   Maximum 4% by weight (laboratory).

**Simple Field Tests:**
Knife Test for Dryness and Compressive Strength.
Drop Test for Dryness and Modulus of Rupture.

### 5. Terrones (Cut Sod Bricks)

(a) Cut sod bricks are widely used in geographic areas where they may be produced. The root structure creates a solid, strong masonry unit. If the bricks are not totally dry however, severe shrinkage and wall settling may occur. The organic material may also attract insects.

(b) Recommend that cut sod bricks be allowed, with the same general conditions and details as of "Untreated Bricks".

## D. Specifications for Treated (Waterproofed) Bricks

Building Code provisions for untreated bricks shall also apply for treated bricks, adding the additional requirements for waterproofing additives that follows.

### 1. Additives

(a) A number of different compounds may be added to the basic mud mixture that will reduce the water erosion and/or absorption of adobe bricks or earth walls. These include, but need not be limited to, portland cement, asphalt emulsion, and various other chemical compounds. Certain indigenous cultures traditionally add natural plant juices and organic materials which at this time have not been identified. At the present time, the most effective and viable compound is asphalt emulsion, in locations where it is available. Quantities required will vary with the soil composition to be used, and may range from as little as 5% or less, to 15% or more. Quantities must be determined by the making of test-brick samples, which can then be tested for waterproof qualities.

(b) Recommend that any admixture be allowed that will limit erosion and/or moisture absorption to suggested limits.

### 2. Testing

(a) Tests for water absorption must be made on sample bricks prepared from the soil to be used, and the necessary quantities of stabilizer will vary from one soil source to another. Partial stabilization, which has some benefits in reducing rain losses, will not provide waterproof qualities required for designation as stabilized bricks.

(b) Recommend that a test be performed

A 4 in. (10 cm) cube cut from a brick should not absorb more than $2\frac{1}{2}$% moisture by weight when placed on a constantly saturated porous surface for 7 days.

### 3. Burned Adobe Bricks (Kiln Fired)

(a) Unstabilized earth bricks that have been dried may be further treated by firing in a simple kiln. The firing will change the chemical composition so they will not erode from water. This will not, however, decrease the moisture absorptive qualities, since the earth bricks may have a substantially lower clay content than standard fired bricks. In geographic areas that experience severe freeze–thaw cycles the surface of the bricks may deteriorate rapidly.

(b) Recommend that the use of burned adobes be allowed, subject to the same limitations as unstabilized earth bricks, and that their exterior use be discouraged in areas with frequent freeze–thaw conditions.

**E. Specifications for Pressed Bricks**

### 1. Manufacturing Method

(a) A number of mechanical devices have been marketed for many years, with which a damp but not wet soil mix is mechanically compacted. Some, such as the Cinva Ram, use a lever arm for compaction. Others, more recently developed, use hydraulic pressure to compact the soil. The latter produces a brick with extremely high compressive strength (1000 psi and more), far in excess of hand made methods (250–400 psi). While the extra strength would seem desirable, problems have developed when certain types of soil are used with high-pressure machines, problems in the form of stresses and expansion of certain types of clay. The expansion may not appear for some time, in some cases after the brick has been placed in the wall, but can lead to serious problems.

(b) Recommend that this type of brick be approved subject to satisfactory testing.

### 2. Soils, Test Bricks

(a) Many types of clay are found in various geographic areas, some of which may be highly expansive when in contact with water or moisture. While the specific clay types may be identified by laboratory analysis, the process is costly, requiring X-ray diffraction tests which may be too expensive to be practical for many projects.

(b) Recommend that sample bricks be made from the specific soils proposed for use, and then tested for expansion when subjected to moisture. If any deformation of the brick occurs, the brick cannot be approved for use.

**F. Mortars**

### 1. Type of Brick

(a) If earth mortar is to be used, it should be of the same material as the brick to provide proper adherence and homogenuity, stabilized or untreated.

(b) Recommend that earth mortars be approved for use if of the same approximate material makeup as the brick, stabilized or untreated.

### 2. Joints

(a) Joints should only be thick enough to accommodate irregularities in brick thickness, and should be placed as solid slush mortar beds. Head joints between the ends of the bricks may be left partially open if the wall is to be plastered, offering additional anchorage for the plaster. Stones in earth mortars that interfere with proper bedding must be removed, by hand or by screening.

(b) Recommend that mortar joints be of minimum thickness to allow proper bedding, full slush type, with partially open head joints allowed if the surface is to be plastered.

### 3. Types of Mortar

(a) Mortar type should be consistent with the type of brick being used, to provide homogenuity, untreated or treated, with same approximate clay content as the bricks. Lime/cement mortars may also be useful to speed laying time or for other purposes.

(b) Recommend that either earth mortars of the same material as the brick or conventional lime/cement mortars such as types M, S, or O be used.

## G. Rammed Earth Walls

Many of the requirements for rammed earth construction will be identical to adobe brick construction and are covered under: structures, foundations, soils for bricks, waterproofing for treated bricks, and plaster and protective coatings.

### 1. Forms

(a) Many types of forms will be suitable for rammed earth wall construction. They may range from patented forming systems to job-built slip forms. Any type of forming system that allows the soil to be compacted to its maximum will be adequate.

(b) Recommend that no limitations be placed on forming systems that will allow full compaction.

### 2. Lifts and Compaction

(a) Uncompacted damp soil shall be compacted in lifts (layers) not to exceed 8 in. (20 cm) to insure maximum compaction. Maximum compaction can be determined simply by a change of sound (ringing) when full compaction has been reached. Most newly compacted earth walls will have a compressive strength of approximately 30–90 psi, which is adequate for most anticipated loads, so that construction may continue uninterrupted.

(b) Recommend that lifts placed in the forms for compaction do not exceed 8 in. (2 cm), and that each lift be compacted to the maximum before the next lift is placed. Each lift shall bond securely with the preceding lift.

### 3. Curing

(a) Rammed earth walls will have an initial compaction strength of approximately 30–90 psi. Curing, or complete drying of the wall, which will increase the compressive strength to 300 psi or more, will take a period of time dependent on wall thickness, temperature, wind, and humidity. The initial compressive strength will be adequate to allow construction to continue as long as loads imposed on it do not exceed that initial compaction strength. This limit is seldom exceeded under most conditions. If structural loads to be imposed will approach or exceed this limit, drying time for the wall must be allowed. It is estimated that drying time will approximate 1½–2 days per in. (2–3 cm) of wall thickness under optimum humidity conditions.

Thus, a 12 in. (30 cm) thick wall will require a minimum of 18–24 days of drying time for curing, with thicker walls requiring a correspondingly longer time. Laboratory tests indicate that strength will increase with time for up to 2 years or more. Compressive strength may be field tested by use of the pocket-knife test (Chapter 4).

(b) Recommend that construction may be continuous unless structural loads approach 30 psi, in which case sufficient curing time should be allowed before such loads are placed on the wall.

## H. Lathing, Plastering, and Protective Coatings

### 1. Cement Stucco

(a) Cement stucco provides a relatively waterproof coating on the apparently vulnerable earth wall surface. Careful observations, though, indicate that the erosion rate of vertical earth surfaces will only approximate 1 in. (2.5 cm) in 20 years, in areas with rainfall to 25 in. (63 cm) per year. While the cement stucco does waterproof the surface to some degree, it can also conceal water and structural damage from other sources. (i.e., roof, flashing, and canal leaks.) Stucco or plaster may prevent wall collapse, even in standing flood water. It must also be noted that the cement stucco, having a different coefficient of expansion than the earth wall, will ultimately separate on exterior surfaces.

(b) Recommend that no requirements be made to use cement stucco unless flood conditions are a serious possibility.

### 2. Thickness

(a) Protective covering (cement stucco or mud plaster) for an earth wall should be a minimum of $\frac{3}{4}$ in. (2 cm) to allow full coverage of irregularities and to allow the application of two or more coats.

(b) Recommend that mud plaster or cement stucco, if used, be applied to a minimum thickness of $\frac{3}{4}$ in. (2 cm).

### 3. Stucco Netting

(a) If cement stucco is used, it should be reinforced with galvanized stucco netting. It is not required for mud plaster or interior plaster surfaces. Cement stucco will have a different coefficient of expansion than earth surfaces, which causes an ultimate separation. Hairline cracks may join to 360° allowing larger areas of stucco to spall from the wall.

(b) Recommend that all exterior cement stucco surfaces be reinforced with galvanized stucco netting, minimum 20 gauge wire, in a 1 in. (2.5 cm) hexagonal pattern, attached to the wall on 16 in. (40 cm) centers with minimum fastener penetration of 1–1$\frac{1}{2}$ in. (4 cm).

### 4. Mud Plaster

(a) Earth plaster is a viable coating for both interior and exterior earth walls. It should be made up of approximately the same balance of sand, silt, and clay as the earth wall, with possibly a slightly higher percentage of clay, and compressed to maximum compaction with a trowel. Its expected life is only slightly less than that of cement stucco, without major repairs, unless damaged by concentrated flows of water from roof drainage, broken pipes, or floods. Flowing water can increase the erosion rate rapidly to failure levels. It requires no reinforcement with stucco netting. Earth plaster may also be stabilized with the same materials used in stabilizing bricks, such as asphalt. If the surface to be plastered is old (oxidized), lack of bonding may require sizing of the surface to increase adhesion.

(b) Recommend that mud plaster be allowed if of the same basic makeup as the earth wall, and no danger of flooding exists.

### 5. Other Coatings

(a) Wash textures, which can be effective and economical, may be used in place of mud plaster or cement stucco. The use of these, however, may increase costs by requiring more uniform masonry work, and complications for additional treatment at door and window frames, bond beams, and mechanical systems. Other penetrating chemical sealers may also be used, although tests of waterproofing and penetrating coatings have shown them to be unsuccessful over long periods of time (2 years or more), and may actually cause increased erosion through spalling of the consolidated waterproofed surfaces. Application of insulation materials on exterior walls usually requires additional protection, such as cement stucco. The insulation manufacturers recommendations should be followed.

(b) Recommend that innovative treatments not in conformance with above requirements be submitted for approval.

It is impossible for all situations to be covered by building-code regulations for earth construction. If a departure is desirable, a request for variance, with supporting information and analysis, should be filed by a responsible party (owner, building contractor, architect or engineer) for approval or modification.

**SUMMARY**

*appendix a*

# New Mexico Building Code for Adobe 1982

The following is an amendment by the State of New Mexico, which replaces Section 2405 of the Uniform Building Code, for "Unburned Clay Masonry." It was adopted in 1982.

**Part V—Engineering Regulations—Quality and Design of Materials of Construction**

CHAPTER 24—MASONRY

UNBURNED CLAY MASONRY

**Sec. 2405.**

(a) *General.* Masonry of unburned clay units shall not be used in any building more than two (2) stories in height. The height of every wall of unburned clay units without lateral support shall be not more than ten (10) times the thickness of such walls. *Exterior* walls, which are laterally supported with those supports located no more than 24 feet apart, are allowed a minimum thickness of 10 inches for single story and a minimum thickness of 14 inches for the bottom story of a two story with the upper story allowed a minimum thickness of 10 inches. *Interior* bearing walls are allowed a minimum thickness of 8 inches. Upward progress of walls shall be in accordance with acceptable practices.

(b) *Soil.* The best way to determine the fitness of a soil is to make a sample brick and allow it to cure in the open, protected from moisture. It should dry without serious warping or cracking. A suitable adobe mixture of sand and clay shall contain not more than 2% of water soluble salts.

(c) *Classes of Earthen Construction*

    (1) *Stabilized Adobes.* The term "stabilized" is defined to mean water resistant adobes made of soils to which certain admixtures are added in the manufacturing process in order to limit the adobe's water absorption. Exterior walls constructed of stabilized mortar and adobe require no additional protection. Stucco is not required. The test required is for a dried four-inch (4″) cube cut from a sample unit shall absorb not more than two and one-half percent moisture by weight when placed upon a constantly water saturated porous surface for seven (7) days. An adobe unit which meets this specification shall be considered "stabilized."

(2) *Untreated Adobes.* Untreated adobes are adobes which do not meet the water absorption specifications. Use of untreated adobes is prohibited within 4 inches above the finished floor grade. Stabilized adobes and mortar may be used for the first 4 inches above finished floor grade. All untreated adobe shall have an approved protection of the exterior walls.

(3) *Hydraulically Pressed Units.* Sample units must be prepared from the specific soil source to be used and may be tested in accordance with approved test procedures.

(4) *Terrones.* The term terrone shall refer to cut sod bricks. Their use is permitted if units are dry and the wall design is in conformance with Sec. 2405 (a).

(5) *Burned Adobe.* The term "burned adobe" shall refer to mud adobe bricks which have been cured by low temperature kiln firing. This type of brick is not generally dense enough to be "frost proof" and may deteriorate rapidly with seasonal freeze-thaw cycles. Its use for exterior locations is discouraged in climate zones with daily freeze-thaw cycles.

(6) *Rammed Earth.*

   1) *Soils:* See Section 2405 (b).

   2) *Moisture Content:* Moisture content of rammed earth walls shall be suitable for proper compaction.

   3) *Forms:* Suitable forms shall be used.

   4) *Lifts and Compaction:* Uncompacted damp soil shall be compacted in lifts not to exceed 6″ until suitable compressive strength is achieved.

   5) *Tests:* Testing of rammed earth construction shall be in accordance with approved standards.

   6) *Curing:* The building officials may allow continuous construction of rammed earth prior to the full curing process, provided proper compaction methods are followed.

(d) *Sampling.* Each of the tests prescribed in this section shall be applied to sample units selected at random at a ratio of 5 units/25,000 bricks to be used or at the discretion of the building official.

(e) *Moisture Content.* The moisture content of untreated units shall be not more than four percent by weight.

(f) *Absorption.* A dried four-inch (4″) cube cut from a sample unit shall absorb not more than two and one-half percent moisture by weight when placed upon a constantly water saturated porous surface for seven (7) days. An adobe unit which meets this specification shall be considered "stabilized".

(g) *Shrinkage Cracks.* No units shall contain more than three shrinkage cracks, and no shrinkage crack shall exceed two inches (2″) in length or one-eighth inch (⅛″) width.

(h) *Compressive Strength.* The units shall have an average compressive strength of 300 pounds per square inch when tested in accordance with ASTM C-67. One sample out of five may have a compressive strength of not less than 250 pounds per square inch.

(i) *Modulus of Rupture.* The unit shall average 50 pounds per square inch in modulus of rupture when tested according to the following procedures:

   1) A standard 4 × 10 × 14 cured unit shall be laid over (cylindrical) supports two inches (2″) from each end, and extending across the full width of the unit.

   2) A cylinder two inches (2″) in diameter shall be laid midway between and parallel to the supports.

   3) Load shall be applied to the cylinder at the rate of 500 pounds per minute until rupture occurs.

   4) The modulus of rupture is equal to $\dfrac{3WL}{2Bd^2}$

      W = Load of rupture
      L = Distance between supports
      B = Width of brick
      d = Thickness of brick

*Footnote:* Tests for pressed units is presently being developed.

(j) *Mortar.* The use of earth mortar is allowed if earth mortar material is of same type as the adobe bricks. Conventional lime/sand/cement mortars of Types M, S, N, are also allowed.

Mortar "bedding" joints shall be full SLUSH type, with partially open "head" joints allowable if surface is to be plastered. All joints shall be bonded (overlapped) a minimum of 4".

(k) *Use.* No adobe shall be laid in the wall dependent on weather conditions until fully cured.

(l) *Foundations.* Adobes shall not be used for foundation or basement walls. All adobe walls, except as noted under Group M Buildings, shall have a continuous concrete footing at least eight inches (8") thick and not less than two inches (2") wider on each side that support the foundation walls above. All foundation walls which support adobe units shall extend to an elevation not less than six inches (6") above the finish grade.

Foundation walls shall be at least as thick as the exterior wall as specified in Section 2405 (l). Where perimeter insulation is used, a variance is allowed for the stem wall width to be two inches (2") smaller than the width of the adobe wall it supports. Alternative foundation systems shall be approved by the building official.

All bearing walls shall be topped with a continuous belt course or tie beam (except patio walls less than 6 feet high above stem). See "o" isolated piers.

(m) *Tie Beams.*
1) *Concrete.* Shall be a minimum of six inches (6") thick by width of top of wall. A bond beam centered to cover $\frac{2}{3}$ of the width of the top of the wall by 6" inch thick shall be allowed for walls wider than 10". All concrete tie beams shall be reinforced with a minimum of two No. 4 reinforcing rods at each floor and ceiling plate line. All bond beam construction shall be in accordance with accepted engineering practices.
2) *Wooden Tie Beam.* Shall be a minimum of 6" wall thickness except as provided for walls thicker than 10" above. Wood tie beams may be solid in the six inch (6") dimension or may be built up by applying layers of lumber. No layer shall be less than one inch (1").

(n) *Wood Lintels.* Shall be minimum in size six inches (6") by wall width. All ends shall have a wall bearing of at least twelve inches (12"). All lintels, wood or concrete, in excess of nine feet (9') shall have specific approval of the building official. The building official shall approve all wooden tie beams for walls thicker than ten inches (10").

(o) *Anchorage.* Roof and floor structures will be suitably anchored to tie beams. Wood joists, vigas or beams shall be spiked to the wood tie beam with large nails or large screws.

Fireplaces shall be secured to the wall mass by suitable ladder reinforcement such as "durowall" or equivalent.

Partitions of wood shall be constructed as specific in Chapter 25, wood and metal partitions may be secured to nailing blocks laid up in the adobe wall or by other approved methods.

(p) *Plastering.* All *untreated* adobe shall have all exterior walls plastered on the outside with Portland cement plaster, minimum thickness $\frac{3}{4}''$ in accordance with Chapter 47. Protective coatings other than plaster are allowed, provided such coating is equivalent to Portland cement plaster in protecting the untreated adobes against deterioration and/or loss of strength due to water. Metal wire mesh minimum 20 guage by one inch (1") opening shall be securely attached to the exterior adobe wall surface by nails or staples with minimum penetration of one and one-half inches ($1\frac{1}{2}''$). Such mesh fasteners shall have a maximum spacing of sixteen inches (16") from each other. All exposed wood surfaces in adobe walls shall be treated with an approved wood preservative before the application of wire mesh. Alternative plastering systems shall be approved by the building official.

EXCEPTION: 1) Exterior patio, yard walls, etc. need not have Portland cement coating.

(q) *Floor Area.* Allowable floor area shall not exceed that specified under Occupancy. Adobe construction shall be allowed the same area as given in Type V-N construction.

(r) *Wall Insulation.* All methods of wall insulation shall comply with the manufacturer's recommendations.

(s) *Stop Work.* The building inspector shall have the authority to issue a stop work order if the provisions of this Section are not complied with.

# Excerpts from 1982 Uniform Building Code

## Unburned Clay Masonry

**Sec. 2405.** (a) **General.** Masonry of stabilized unburned clay units shall not be used in any building more than one story in height. The unsupported height of every wall of unburned clay units shall be not more than ten times the thickness of such walls. Bearing walls shall in no case be less than 16 inches. All footing walls which support masonry of unburned clay units shall extend to an elevation not less than 6 inches above the adjacent ground at all points.

(b) **Units.** At the time of laying, all units shall be clean and damp at the surface and shall have been stabilized with emulsified asphalt in accordance with U.B.C. Standard No. 24-14.

(c) **Laying.** All joints shall be solidly filled with Type M or S mortar. Bond shall be provided as specified for masonry of hollow units in Section 2410.

(d) **Stresses.** All masonry of unburned clay units shall be so constructed that the unit stresses do not exceed those set forth in Table No. 24-B. Bolt values shall not exceed those set forth in Table No. 24-C.

# Index

**Index**